Max's Picnic Book

Max Halley & Ben Benton

Hardie Grant

BOOKS

This is not
It is a book a

cookbook.
bout picnics.

**For Ned, Sheila and Lydia,
forever and always.**

Introduction

Originally a good excuse for a few drinks outdoors, the picnic has since been ripped from its roots, chewed up, spat out and then stamped to death by art, literature, movies and cynical branding. Instead of being fun and achievably delicious, the picnic has become chintzy and dunked in rose-tinted, wasp-attracting goo. Enid Blyton-esque abominations such as homemade ginger beer, bunting and sweaters for goalposts have become part of the collective conscience's perception of the thing.

Even feeling as I do, I find myself accidentally complicit in the picnic's great identity crisis of the early twenty-first century. Closing my eyes and imagining one, I can't help but be in a stately home's garden where vivid green trees and verdant hedgerows abound. The sun is shining, blankets are spread everywhere and people in peach-coloured clothing are saying things like 'Scrum-diddly-umptious!' and 'These cucumber sandwiches are simply sensational.'

As a species we have been picnicking since we came out of the slime. A little light lunch next to the dead Woolly Mammoth? Picnic. Some scraps pinched from outside the neighbour's cave? Picnic. Lunch on the train or at your desk? Picnic. Dinner in the car park of a motorway service station at 1 a.m.? PICNIC GODAMMIT!

By the eighteenth century, the *pique-nique*, taking its name from the gluttonous character in a bawdy French satire of 1649, had become an (indoor) jolly, where guests brought their own culinary contributions. In 1748 a young Lord Chesterfield found himself partying in a garden somewhere outside Leipzig. He wrote to his father (Earl Chesterfield, he of the sofa) and described the day's events as a picnic, coining the term in English.

The picnic cantered through culture at such pace that by 1801, a Pic Nic Society had been founded in London's Fitzrovia. Legendarily raucous, their meetings were a mash up of lunch, dinner, serious prolonged heavy drinking and shonky amateur dramatics. The society's rulebook specified that all attendees arrive at the venue with one item of food, and six bottles of wine.

The Society's star burned bright, but brief and in 1802, Richard Brinsley Sheridan, a greedy, influential playwright and the owner of the Drury Lane Theatre, worried that the group's antics were eating into his market share and had the authorities shut them down.

I am telling you this, not to furnish you with historical dullness, but to remind you that the picnic hasn't always been the *Sound of Music* bullsh!t we know it as today. When I think of what the poor picnic has become, I want to run for the hills, hills which are alive not with the sound of music, but the sound of screaming.

This most malleable and moveable of feasts, the picnic, is for us all, the many not the few and together, we must take it back. We must crush the marketeers who sell us unnecessary wicker baskets and *Wind in the Willows* fantasies. When we see a pickled egg in a bag of crisps with some of the pub's Tabasco tipped in it, 'PICNIC!' we shall cry. When we see a Thermos flask of scrambled eggs whipped out on a train? 'PICNIC!' we shall roar again with our arms in the air.

There does not have to be fizzy pop, Scotch eggs, sausage rolls and an allegedly innovative approach to hummus for a picnic to be a picnic. You should be able to sit at your desk at work, smash your way through a flask of hot, tinned beef consommé with a packet of store-bought ravioli tipped in it, and think of yourself quite rightly, as a picnicker of great repute.

If this book achieves its goal, next time you're in town having some fast food, you'll remember there's a miniature bottle of whisky in your bag and order some pudding accordingly: 'A large

vanilla milkshake and a double espresso, please.'
You will sling the coffee and the miniature into the
milkshake, stir it all about and walk down the street,
tripping the light fantastic, slurping your Irish
coffee and shouting out loud for all to hear: 'My
name is ...! And I am PICNICKING LIKE A BOSS!'

Max & Ben

The following sixteen fictional picnic stories and accompanying menus are, both in content and spirit, utterly fantastical. Their threads metaphorically demonstrate the ways in which we can rethink what the picnic really is, while paying homage to our real (and imaginary) heroes.

So, as a disclaimer, I would like to mostly quote the great Trey Parker and Matt Stone, creators of *South Park*:

All characters and events in this book, even those based on real people and occasions, are entirely fictitious. It is full of coarse language, casual sex and drug references, and many really bad jokes. As a result of these things, we recommend it should not be read by anyone.

Life is full of
for delic

Picnic li

opportunities

ousness.

e a boss!

An 'Opportunity for Deliciousness' Picnic

To misquote Dale Carnegie: 'A picnic isn't what you eat, who is there, where it takes place or what goes down – it's how you think about it. A pickled egg in a bag of crisps is still a picnic.'

'Venerate, don't emulate' – that's how my mum told me to handle rogues and my lunatic heroes. Whatever the inspiration, we must always remember to picnic with our own style and panache. To feel free consuming whatever we want, wherever we like, be that a bottle of Chivas Regal and a packet of Dunhill on a park bench, or a forkful of quiche on a nice gingham blanket.

I very much hope you are familiar with today's host. Much was made, mostly by him, of Hunter S. Thompson's love of drugs, alcohol and gun-based violence. Behind the bravado, though, was one of the most brilliant, brutal, sabre-like minds of his generation. His suspicion and understanding, or as he put it, 'fear and loathing', of America's political establishment gave him an ability to see through the fog and the lies, to look plainly and with terrifying accuracy at the misery, horror and evil cantering through the sky towards him, dressed up as politics. As for Hunter's imaginary picnic companion, we have arguably the most beloved Mary of all, Mary Berry. For the unanointed, she is Britain's Grande Dame de Demerara, our Queen's Counsel of Sugar and Butter – and in (vanilla) essence, a British Martha Stewart or Maggie Beer.

MENU

All-day Breakfast Quiche

Pickled Eggs

Packet of Crisps and Available Condiments

A Bottle of Chivas Regal

Rosé wine

At least 20 Dunhills

Fantasy Host
Hunter S. Thompson

Fantasy Guest
Mary Berry

Location
Your nearest park bench. That's all you need for a picnic, baby.

Dress Code
Sunglasses

Unpacking the Hamper

I found a great old video on the internet where Mary Berry talks about her picnic techniques. She extols the virtues of making a stack of sandwiches earlier in the week, freezing them whole and defrosting them in a cooler bag on the way to *La Grande Bouffe*. Venerate, don't emulate, I said before. Venerate, don't emulate.

Thankfully today she has followed her heart, not her admittedly practical head, and whipped up an All-day Breakfast Quiche (page 26).

'I got the idea from my dear friend Joan Lee,' she says, 'mother of infamous cheese fiend Holly Chaves. Joan's quiche is, as dear LL Cool J would say ... A PHENOMENON!!!'.

To set the scene of this fantasy picnic, imagine Hunter and Mary parking 'The Red Shark' (Hunter's car, a red 1973 Chevrolet Caprice, which he certainly put the capricious in), then ambling hand in hand into the park like Winnie the Pooh and Piglet into the Hundred Acre Wood, looking for a spot for lunch. And somewhere for Hunter to get a drink pronto tonto, of course. They pass beneath a blossoming horse chestnut tree and, in a moment of serendipity, emerge from its boughs in front of a gorgeous pub in the middle of the park.

'Quick pre-prandial refreshment, Mary?' Hunter asks with a wry smile.

While Mary settles herself on a stool at the bar, Hunter orders, and dispatches, a quadruple whiskey, then realises he's in need of a snack. 'You got chips?' he asks the barman in true Louisville, Kentucky form.

'Crisps?' the bloke says. 'We do. What flavour?'

'The nearest ones,' Hunter answers, scanning the back of the bar... 'I've been to England before,' he says, 'I know your pubs, you always got Tabasco and Worcestershire Sauce.' *Plonk* – a pair of faded bottles land in front of him. The Tabasco, brown from years of neglect, still tastes perfect; and the Lea & Perrins, probably *in situ* since the seventies, has been – and will stay – just the same until well into the next millennium. Hunter takes the lids off the two bottles, picks them up in one hand and – *shploof, shploof* – gives his crisps both barrels.

He gives the bag a little crush with his hand and says, 'Slam me one of those pickled eggs in here too, will ya? Straight in the bag.' He turns to Mary. 'Drink, dear?'

'Vodka tonic, please. I see you've just turned a packet of crisps and a pickled egg into a picnic.'

'Have I?' Hunter wonders. 'Sure, I guess I did. I'm a damn natural. Life is full of opportunities for deliciousness my dear, and we must grasp every one of them.'

Mary, with plans of her own, asks the barman if he has any Scampi Fries. Joyfully, they do. She opens the bag, gives him a quid, takes the lemon slice from her empty glass and squeezes it into the crisps. The barman's had enough, WHO ARE THESE LEGENDS?

Mary grabs the cooler bag and Scampi Fries in hand, arm slunk through Hunter's, they wander back into the daylight outside. They find a park bench under a shady tree. From the cooler bag, Mary whips out the picnic kitbag (page 23) that's kept in The Red Shark's glovebox: it's an old washbag containing a bottle of Tabasco, some other rotating condiments (often HP and horseradish sauce), two sets of cutlery, a Victorinox penknife, two Duralex tumblers, and an inordinate number of napkins. Isn't she just the best?! She's some kind of Picnic Superhero! Fret not, though – you can be too. Keep this stuff in your car's glovebox and every motorway service station from now on will be an opportunity to 'picnic like a boss'.

Hunter's started his Scotch and is merrily guzzling away, Dunhill on the go. Mary's got herself a glass of rosé and a thick wedge of quiche, which she has doused with a sachet of brown sauce she found in the kitbag.

'What's the brown goo?' Hunter asks, deeply mystified by Mary's display of park-based condiment confidence.

'Try some,' she says, 'it's lovely with a sausage.'

'Sh!t, that's delicious!' he shouts. 'It's like A1 Steak Sauce, but thicker. And better.'

Hunter makes an excellent point. A1 Sauce you see, is made with raisin purée, while his new favourite HP Sauce is made with the sweeter, deeper, richer date and its good friend tamarind.

With their pimped-up crisps and condimented quiche, these two heroes have demonstrated the very essence of picnicking: they have made the most of an opportunity for deliciousness, with whatever is available. Deliciousness isn't about Michelin stars, being 'in the know' or over-intellectualising lunch, thought about right – admittedly sometimes loitering in the dark – deliciousness is everywhere and often in the most unexpected of places.

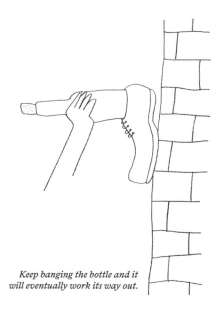

Keep banging the bottle and it will eventually work its way out.

Pack your own

If you can't be arsed to make a quiche, just buy one. I think the little Lorraines the supermarkets sell aren't half bad – and anyway, once you've covered it in the hot sauce and brown sauce you now have in your car's glovebox, who cares? After you have quiched to your heart's delight and filled your boots with crisps and pickled eggs, all there is left to do is get really, really drunk on whisky in the park and try and smoke a whole pack of cigarettes.

HACKS

Nine essentials for your keep-in-the-glovebox road-trip picnic kitbag

1   Condiments: Tabasco (or other) hot sauce; Worcestershire sauce; Henderson's Relish and any other favourites, a small bottle of vinegar (I go malt), bottled lemon juice (for livening up a Coca-Cola or a grim bag of salad) and a selection of booze miniatures (not for the driver, obviously!); perhaps a bottle of Tajín seasoning too ...

2   Sachets of salt (and sauces): either pinched from fast-food outlets, or homemade wraps of salt mixed with delicious things (page 167).

3   Always keep napkins from your takeaway. Same goes for wet wipes.

4   One Victorinox penknife.

5   Two little empty plastic bottles: I have one full of lime cordial for tipping into big bottles of sparkling water.

6   Two (ideally) windproof lighters.

7   Pomegranate molasses: unexpectedly useful – there aren't many things that are just as good on salad or grilled meats as they are in a milkshake or with ice cream.

8   Two Duralex glasses and a small Thermos flask.

9   Two small, clean Tupperware containers, for eating out of ...

Joan Lee's
All-day Breakfast Quiche

To have a full English breakfast at a picnic (which is definitely something you *do* want to have), you have to do one of two things. You can either fill a bun, roll or two bits of bread with all the constituent parts, wrap it and pack it and take it with you on your picnic, or, you think like Joan Lee, a culinary maven, and pack the breakfast staples into a pastry case, cover it in eggs and cream, bake it and take it with you wherever you may be going.

Serves 4–6

320 g (11¼ oz) ready-rolled
   shortcrust pastry
6 free-range eggs
300 ml (10 fl oz/1 ¼ cups) double
   (heavy) cream
8 cooked pork sausages

12 rashers smoked streaky bacon,
   cooked until crisp
4 ripe tomatoes, halved and fried
   in bacon fat until soft
100 g (3½ oz) mushrooms of your
   choice, roughly chopped
Salt and freshly ground black pepper

Preheat the oven to 180°C (350°F/gas 4).

Unfurl the pre-rolled pastry and flop it into a tart tin. Use whatever style of tin you have; if you need to change the shape of your pastry, trim and cut and reshape as needed. At the end of the day all you want is a tart tin with pastry completely covering the inside, if it looks like Frankenstein's tart case, so be it, you're never going to see it again once it's filled and cooked.

Once lined, cover the pastry case with a piece of baking parchment, add some dry beans, rice, chickpeas, baking beans or clean stones and place in the hot oven for 10–15 minutes to blind bake the pastry. Check after 10 minutes: you are looking for a firm biscuity pastry, not sweaty flabby pastry. If it needs longer, give it longer, checking every 3–4 minutes. Once biscuity and just colouring, remove the baking beans and the parchment and give the case a final 2 minute flourish in the oven.

Meanwhile, mix your eggs and cream in a jug and whisk together, then cook your full English as you normally would. I would recommend; streaky bacon into a cold pan, onto a medium heat, slowly cooked until starting to crisp, you'll want to stop short of your full on crispy bacon; sausages cooked in the oven until golden brown; tomatoes halved, seasoned with salt and pepper and cooked in the bacon pan once the bacon is cooked; and finally, sliced mushrooms fried hard with a small pinch of salt in the tomatoey bacon fat until dark and gloriously defeated.

One you have your baked tart case and your cooked breakfast, all you have to do is layer. I like to lay the sausages in the base of the tart case. Push the tomato halves into the spaces between the sausages. Scatter the mushrooms over this, then pour over the creamy egg mixture allowing it to find and fill all the holes and cavities amongst the bits and pieces. Finally, press your bacon rashers into the surface of the quiche and return the whole thing to the oven to cook for 20–25 minutes until the egg is almost completely set to a reluctant wobble and the surface has a nice browny-bubbly finish.

Allow to cool for 20–30 minutes before slicing and serving. Brown sauce is a must with this; hot sauce is highly recommended.

Brown Sauce, aka Picnic Gold

If you're making Joan Lee's All-day Breakfast Quiche, you'd be a mug not to also make your own tart and fruity brown sauce. This is picnic gold. Sharper and livelier than HP sauce, this sits somewhere between a condiment and a chutney, with the best parts of both. A puddle of this stuff is enough to enliven any meal, even a store-bought quiche or savoury pastry. And don't be alarmed by the long list of ingredients. You just cook a bit of onion and then bang everything else in, it couldn't be simpler.

Makes about 1.5 litres (50 fl oz/6 cups)

2 tablespoons olive oil
2 onions, finely chopped
1 teaspoon salt
15 g (½ oz) ginger, peeled and
    finely grated
1 bay leaf
1 star anise
2 cloves
12 grinds of black pepper
5 juniper berries

½ teaspoon fennel seeds
¼ teaspoon ground allspice
2 tablespoons Worcestershire sauce
2 tablespoons black treacle (molasses)
2 x 400 g (14 oz) tins of plum tomatoes,
    juice and all
150 g (5 oz) shop-bought apple sauce
500 ml (17 fl oz/2 cups) stout
50 g (2 oz) dates, chopped
100 ml (3½ fl oz) red wine vinegar

Gather and prepare all your ingredients before you start cooking. You want it all laid out before you.

Place a heavy-based saucepan over a medium heat and add your oil to the pan. When it is hot, add the onions and salt and cook, stirring occasionally, for 10–15 minutes. This bit is important: you will get a deep, sweet flavour from this low and slow cooking. When your onions are completely soft and starting to brown, add the ginger and cook for 3 minutes. Next add the bay leaf and all the spices, stirring and cooking for another 3 minutes, or until you can smell their heady aroma.

At this point, increase the heat and add the rest of your ingredients except the vinegar. Bring to the boil, reduce to a gentle simmer and let it bubble away for 45 minutes, stirring occasionally. You want the sauce to reduce and go nice and dark and thick. Finally, stir in the vinegar. Taste the sauce: if you want to enhance the flavours, adjust the salt; if you want it sharper, add a little more vinegar.

When you are happy, leave the sauce to cool before passing it through a sieve to remove the whole spices. When completely cool, pour into sterilised jars or bottles and keep in the fridge – it keeps for months and makes an excellent present.

Homemade Pickled Eggs

If you've never popped a pickled egg into a packet of salt and vinegar crisps and given the whole thing a bit of a scrunch before eating, then you're the sort of wrong 'un we normally try to avoid. But you've purchased this book and you're reading this recipe, so actually, you're gold.

A pickled egg is a versatile thing. Yes, they are a rarefied treat as described above, but they're also a great way to knock up a lightning-speed egg mayo sandwich with a nice little kick, and a bona-fide snack in their own right. You can add all manner of aromatics to the pickling vinegar and you'll have a new spin on the humble pickled egg. A couple of tablespoons of soy and mirin can take you down a very naughty path, as can a jalapeño or two. We'll leave it to you to experiment.

Makes 12

12 medium free-range eggs,
  at room temperature
2 sprigs of thyme
2 bay leaves

A few whole black peppercorns
About 500 ml (17 fl oz/2 cups)
  distilled vinegar

Bring a saucepan of water to the boil. Gently spoon the eggs into the pan and simmer for exactly 7 minutes before running the pan under the cold tap until the eggs are cool enough to handle.

Peel off the shells and pack the eggs into a sterilised Kilner (Mason) jar or similar container (you'll want something that's airtight and big enough to hold all the eggs snugly). Add the thyme, bay leaves and peppercorns, then pour in enough vinegar to completely cover the eggs.

Seal the container and leave the eggs to mature for at least a week before popping one in a bag of crisps and seeing what happens. Remember, never put your fingers in the pickle jar! Use a spoon to retrieve your beautiful friends.

A Raw Picnic

Be bold in your mismatching of food and venue: you never know where true synchronicity might come from.

This picnic is inspired by those moments when no picnic was intended. The assembled gang seem unusual, but by opening our minds and taking a punt in life, we often end up having a wonderful, wonderful time. To increase our chances of picnic-based happiness, we must be ready to adapt and react, something our host, Genghis Khan, considers himself a poster boy for. At this picnic, he has his heart set on something that sounds impossibly mismatched with the occasion: steak tartare.

Continuing the theme of ingenuity, we have two Parkers, Dorothy and Bonnie, who both have a knack for turning something basic – little gem, tinned seafood and a jar of mayonnaise, in this case – into something beautiful. As for Oscar Wilde, it is open to debate whether he was an original thinker, a plagiarist or just plain disingenuous when he proclaimed, 'I can't stand people who do not take food seriously.' The point is, an unexpected picnic, particularly when it involves raw, seasoned meat, is a wonderful thing indeed.

Steak Tartare

Seafood Salad Cups

Perfect 'Arnold Palmer' Iced Tea

Fantasy Host
Genghis Khan

Fantasy Guests
Dorothy Parker, Bonnie Parker and Oscar Wilde

Location

Given Genghis's extraordinary riding skills, we would say somewhere horse-friendly, but as so few places have bridleways and tethering posts these days, it just seems silly. Cycling is a more modern joy and if you live in a city, beautiful spots are easily reachable if you get on a train with your bike. Once you're out of town, as long as there's room to plump your cushions and have a lie down, all you need is a lovely tree for shade and a powerful speaker for playing inconsiderately loud music.

Dress Code

We will never know if it was discussed beforehand, but not one of our fantasy picnickers is wearing underwear.

Unpacking the Hamper

Steak tartare, seafood salad cups and an Arnold Palmer? You may not think these three things are natural bedfellows, but you wouldn't have thought that of our little picnic group either, would you? How on earth did such a group of people come together? Well, pull up that blanket, have another sip of tea, wiggle your toes and I'll tell you.

Had you heard Dorothy and Bonnie Parker getting their bikes out of the shed this morning, you'd have heard a great deal of swearing. Two bikes, two flat tyres? COME ON …

From a young age, Bonnie Parker wrote poetry, displayed great affection for literature and daydreamed about being a movie star. I suppose nothing makes a child dream of a star-spangled future like growing up in a town called Cement City. If what Neil Young said is true, and it is better to burn out than fade away, Bonnie Parker did just fine. She largely achieved her goals by becoming extremely famous, and oddly, kind of adored. A rebel hero, despite her and Clyde's reputation, she never actually killed anyone – she liked to watch.

Had her circumstances been different, and had she been exposed to a less criminal world from such a young age, might she have become something closer to Dorothy Parker? Despite being one of the most highly regarded writers, poets and satirists of her day, Dorothy Parker was never happy – and if she was, she never let on. What with her self-deprecating pieces about her disastrous love life and dependence on drink, I can't help but wonder if she was somehow destined for sadness. 'I don't care what's written about me' she said, 'as long as it isn't true.'

When Bonnie and Dorothy's dreams of a cycle down shade-dappled lanes were temporarily dashed this morning, they dropped their bikes in for repairs and hit the pub. Three minutes in, they got talking to two lads at the bar. One, the gregarious and boisterous Genghis Khan and the other, his louche, lounge-lizard companion, Oscar Wilde. On discovering a mutual love of the picnic, the group decided to lunch together.

The occasion may be lacking the 'car keys in a bowl' frisson Genghis generally looks for, but the idea of a culinary mash up of sorts and the pleasures it might hold, has got them all chomping at the bit. After years on the rampage, Genghis likes his food raw. He, and many of the Tartars he conquered, allegedly invented steak tartare by tucking a horse or yak steak beneath their saddles. They would end up with a piece of meat not only tenderised by the rider's impact, but seasoned with the horse's sweat. Genius.

With their menu decided, the gang park their newly fixed bikes outside a convenience store and head in. The two Parkers roam the aisles like Genghis on the plains. They find jars of pickled cockles and mussels, packets of prawns, smoked mackerel, posh tinned tuna and many other lovely things. Remembering the mayonnaise she has in her pannier, Bonnie's over the moon: 'We can mix all this fishy gear into some of my mayonnaise,' she shouts. 'Stick it in a lettuce cup with a squeeze of lemon juice and we're in like Flynn.'

Genghis is keen to add a bit of the Tabasco and horseradish he keeps in his picnic kitbag too, an idea one can assume he's picked up from a friend (page 23).

Oscar wonders if he might make a round or two of cucumber sandwiches and Bonnie says he can do whatever he likes. Because cheap bread makes Bonnie bloated, she's very chuffed with the potential versatility of these lettuce cups for being able to eat seafood salad, steak tartare or just about anything else of that sort that normally requires bread.

Coming across a lovely spot beneath a weeping willow, the gang park up and prepare to lunch. Due to an old riding injury, Genghis prefers not to sit directly on the ground. He whips off his robe and rolls it into a cushion, revealing one of his greatest coups. He's been on eBay and somehow found a rare 2019 KFC polo-shirt picnic blanket. The gang also notice he's sporting the KFC x Crocs collaboration and no one quite knows what to say. Bonnie makes a joke about the Crocs, Genghis looks hurt, and Dorothy points out that Bonnie should be a bit nicer because 'beauty is only skin deep, but ugly goes clean to the bone'.

For drinks, Genghis is certain that nothing livens the stomach and one's outlook quite like yak blood and milk, particularly once it has begun to ferment. Somehow, allegedly accidentally, Oscar has brought Genghis' Thermos of black tea instead of his yak's bladder full of blood and milk. He also has their shared Thermos, which is filled with ice-cold, homemade lemonade. Bonnie says that back in Texas every household has a jug of sweetened iced tea in the chiller for unexpected guests. Oscar thinks himself a genius when he has the idea of mixing his lemonade with Genghis' fast-cooling tea. Dorothy, who can spot a cocktail at a hundred paces (even a boozeless one), points out that the drink already exists and it's called an Arnold Palmer, telling Oscar that were he to throw some vodka in there, it would be a John Daly.

Seemingly from nowhere, Dorothy produces a martini glass and a Thermos of her own. Sneaking one of the cornichons Genghis has for his tartare, she pours an ice-cold wet-martini into the glass, pops in the pickle and puts her feet up on a log as she watches the birds ducking and weaving on the breeze, sipping her Cornichon Gibson.

Pack your own

Little gem is the best of all the lettuces: diminutive, well cupped and with a pleasing hint of bitterness, the leaves make a perfect vehicle for all kinds of things. If you are using tinned fish in your seafood cocktails, especially if it is of Spanish or Portuguese origin, add some of the tin's oily liquor to the mayo – it is infused with the flavour of whatever it's been in the tin with. For steak tartare, we recommend popping down to the butcher's shop on your way to your chosen venue, asking them to do the chopping (never mincing, always chopping), and then assembling the dish on site. Lastly, never forget Bonnie's golden rule: 'Anything mixed into mayonnaise is delicious. Especially in a salad cup'. Over and out.

HACKS

Eight reasons you should definitely have a Swiss Army Knife in your picnic kitbag

1 It can cut through ANYTHING (the saw is great for bread) and it's got pliers.

2 You can do your nails in the park.

3 If so inclined, you can dispatch and neatly eviscerate an animal for a real woodland picnic ... (joking).

4 It will be MADLY useful in MILLIONS of ways none of us have even thought of yet.

5 It has a corkscrew, a bottle opener AND a can opener, meaning that there is no beverage on the planet it cannot open.

6 You could get 'Happy Picnicking Babes, Love From Me' engraved on the blade and make a romantic pressie out of it.

7 It is indispensable for picking wild flowers and taking cuttings of plants (where permitted!) to take home as a beautiful, if ephemeral, souvenir of your day out.

8 If it's good enough for MacGyver ...

Steak Tartare

This is a sensational recipe, whether you're making it at home or out and about. If you want to tartare at your picnic and haven't successfully persuaded your butcher to chop the meat up for you, you'd better have a penknife in that kitbag and have remembered a chopping board.

Makes enough for 8–10 lettuce cups

200 g (7 oz) beef (ideally something lean, such as fillet)

2 little gem (bibb) lettuces, leaves separated

Seasoning ingredients
1 shallot, finely diced
1 teaspoon white wine vinegar or lemon juice

1 tablespoon capers, finely chopped
1 teaspoon ground black pepper
½ teaspoon salt
½ teaspoon Dijon mustard
Optional extras (not really, you'd be mad not to use these too): 1 egg yolk, a small handful of chopped parsley and a dash of Tabasco sauce

Chop your steak at home, add all the seasoning ingredients and mix well, then store in an airtight container until you are ready to eat.

If you are heading out on a hot day, you might not want to carry a bag full of raw meat, gently sweating in its own juices. On such a day, it's a good idea to mix all the seasoning ingredients at home and take them with you in a little tub. While out and about, purchase your chosen piece of steak from a butcher, ask them to finely chop (never mince) the meat for you, and then mix the seasonings into the meat just before you eat.

Either way, when the time cones, simply spoon the tartare into the lettuce cups and serve with the 'optional' extras alongside.

Why not explore the butcher's counter a little further? Much of the cow works well in this way, be it as beef or veal. Heart is a world-beater when tartared, with some expert commentators (Ben Benton) suggesting it makes a steakier-tasting steak tartare than steak does. People are funny about heart, but it's not a creepy secreting/filtering organ like liver or kidneys, it's just a muscle like rump or fillet.

Seafood Cocktail

If you want to go the full bunger, seek out some lovely little jars of pickled seafood – they're made by Parsons and come all the way from Wales. Their seafood is high-welfare etc., yadda yadda, but most importantly, it is delicious. You can, of course, make this with other tinned seafood or even 400 g (14 oz) of straight-up regular prawns. That would be delicious. If you want to do that, just make the sauce as described below and then mix your prawns through – you might like to add a little red wine vinegar to the sauce, too, as you won't have the benefit of the pickling liquor from the jars of seafood.

**Makes enough for 2 massive sandwiches,
4 seafood cocktails or 12–15 lettuce cups**

300 g (10½ oz) i.e. 2 x 155 g (5¼ oz)
 jars pickled seafood, such as cockles
 or mussels
100 g (3½ oz) cooked brown shrimps,
 prawns or crayfish tails
2 little gem (bibb) lettuces
Chives and cayenne pepper,
 to serve (optional)

For the cocktail sauce
6 tablespoons good mayonnaise,
 preferably Hellmann's, Kewpie
 or Duke's
2 tablespoons tomato ketchup
2 teaspoons Worcestershire sauce
½ teaspoon cayenne pepper
Loads of Tabasco sauce
Juice of ½ lemon
A splash of brandy (optional)

Drain the pickled seafood, but keep the liquid.

To make the sauce, combine the mayo, ketchup, Worcestershire sauce, cayenne, Tabasco, lemon juice (and brandy) and 1–2 tablespoons of the pickling liquid in a large bowl. Mix well, taste and tweak – it can take more Tabasco than you think. When you are happy with your sauce, add the seafood and stir to coat. That's it.

If you are sandwiching, liberally butter both pieces of bread, cram as much seafood on as possible, top with shredded little gem lettuce, an extra squeeze of lemon juice and ponder what flavour crisp (potato chip) to crush up and sprinkle on. Prawn cocktail would seem too good a trick to miss.

If you are lettuce cupping, carefully separate the leaves, discarding any rotters and removing any mud. Dollop tablespoonfuls of saucy seafood into each cup. Dust with cayenne and sprinkle with chives if you fancy it. When you get down to the core leaves of the lettuce that are too small to use as a cup, you could not use them, eat them there and then, or shred them and mix them into the sauce. Which is what I would do.

Perfect 'Arnold Palmer' Iced Tea

Arnold Palmer was a golfer with a languid swing and a diamond-cut palate for iced tea. As such, he gave his name to this, the most refreshing of all non-alcoholic drinks – and we include water and Mountain Dew in that list.

Makes enough for 4 large glasses

20 g (¾ oz) loose-leaf black tea or 3 tea bags
100 g (3½ oz) caster (superfine) sugar
Juice of 2 lemons, plus slices to serve
Angostura Bitters (optional)

Put the tea or tea bags into a jug or spouted receptacle with 600 ml (21 fl oz/ 2½ cups) of cold water. Cold water, and a long brew (3–4 hours before straining) makes the tea less tannic and bitter. If you are in a rush, brew the tea in 600ml (21 fl oz/2 ½ cups) of freshly boiled water for 3 minutes if using loose-leaf tea, or 1 minute if using tea bags, then sieve it and decant it into an old mineral water bottle or something – the cold method is much better.

For the lemonade, put 75 ml (3 fl oz/ ⅓ cup) of tap water into a pan and bring it to the boil and take off the heat. Add the sugar and stir slowly and carefully until completely dissolved. Allow to cool, stir in the lemon juice and add 600 ml (21 fl oz /2 ½ cups) of tap water. I do this in a spouted bowl, then funnel it into an old water bottle that the tea will fit in too.

You can keep the tea and the lemonade separate in case your chosen ratio of lemonade to tea changes. Iced tea and homemade lemonade are very personal things. You might prefer the tea much stronger or the lemonade much sweeter, so experiment with how you like it and remember to write your recipe down.

Arnold Palmer is at its best served in a huge glass, full of ice, with a slice of lemon. and possibly a couple of drops of some Angostura Bitters.

3

'The use of an iconic food in an act of violence ... is reprehensible ... Hot dogs are meant to be enjoyed – not weaponized.' Janet Riley - President of the National Hot Dog and Sausage Council (USA)

In the long-lost bucolic Britain of my youth, you couldn't shake a stick in the summer without hitting a sports day of some kind. Grass so green, clothes so white and competition so fierce, I remember the terror of school sports days as vividly as I remember Ben Johnson and his eyes in the 1988 Olympic 100-metres final.

The food at these events was always awful. Mostly churned out by the school canteen or the vicar's wife or something, there was invariably a massive plastic container of lukewarm cordial and, if you were lucky, some melted chocolate biscuits. The only hope of salvation was that someone's mum might have packed a few extra sweaty sandwiches.

Don't think for a moment we're here to relive those picnic though! We've upped our game. That's why this picnic brings together sporting legends and a sporting event legend – the hot dog. As revered skier Jean-Claude Killy will go on to show us, the ultimate sports day picnic food, is BLATANTLY the frankfurter. Equally attractive unadorned, or smothered in condiments, this most versatile of meat-treats is satisfying, filling, delicious and wonderfully nostalgic; everything a sports day picnic could and should have been …

MENU

Hot Dogs in Homemade Potato Rolls

Green Chilli

DIY Toppings

Guinness Cocktails

Fantasy Host
Jean-Claude Killy

Fantasy Guests
Michael Jordan, Serena Williams, Bobby George, Fatima Whitbread, Diego Maradona, Alex 'Hurricane' Higgins

Location
A wide-open, grassy space where no one will be upset by the sound of a starting pistol.

Dress Code
Tracksuits and trainers; no running spikes, though – that's cheating.

Unpacking the Hamper

I believe that Jean-Claude Killy, one of sport's great tacticians, would doubtless have done a deal with Trangia for a portable stove here, so he could heat up his franks and toast his buns in the park like a (snow) baller – but really all you need to make like a sports star and reinvent the wiener is a gang of mates, a Thermos flask of boiling water, some paper plates and a trip to the shops.

At this fantasy picnic, Jean-Claude Killy has brought a case of hot dogs in jars: 12 jars, 8 hot dogs in each, 96 hot dogs in total. Thank God he isn't relying solely on that Trangia and told everyone to bring a Thermos of boiling water (something you should consider doing, too). In one slalom-whizz round the supermarket, Killy has curated a connoisseur's collection of condiments: ketchup, French's mustard, Kewpie mayo, lime pickle, hot sauce of every colour, brown sauce, curry sauce, maple syrup, Maggi, Lea & Perrins ... the list goes on.

Serena Williams loves tacos – who doesn't? When Killy asked her to bring toppings for the dogs he had planned, she decided to think about garnishing them taco-style. She thought about layering up textures and flavours, keeping the Max's Sandwich Mantra never far from her mind: Hot, Cold, Sweet, Sour, Crunchy, Soft, the secret of deliciousness.

Serena's got crispy onions, soft, slow cooked onions, lime pickled onions (lime juice and salt put on a sliced red onion, chucked in a Tupperware and shaken violently every so often for a day or two), sauerkraut, guacamole, crushed crisps (potato chips), Bombay mix, piccalilli, pickled jalapeños, grated cheese, coriander (cilantro) and a host of other things to boot.

Maradona nails his straight off the bat by doing what everyone should do, and thinking of his sausage as a Reuben sandwich. He's got sauerkraut, mustard, cheese, crispy onions and hot sauce. It's Fatima Whitbread, though, who wins the gang's hearts when she shows the ultimate restraint and simply goes double sausage, a line of French's and a small sprinkling of green chilli.

Time for drinks! Bobby and Maradona rummage in Killy's cooler bags and find cans of Guinness, bottles of Champagne, Tia Maria miniatures, vodka, a huge bottle of bourbon and, underneath all that, even more Guinness.

The gang are everywhere, tipping Tia Marias and shots of bourbon into their Guinnesses when Bobby George has a brainwave and shouts 'BLACK VELVETS! RAZZMATAZZ!'. He just over half-fills glasses with Champagne and slowly tops them up with Guinness. Do it in that order and it won't fizz up so bad. He hands them round to everyone and the party really gets started. Cheap Cava would be a PERFECT substitute for the Champers here, but NO BLOODY PROSECCO!

Would Hurricane Higgins have enjoyed this picnic? Nestled in the bosom of the party, among such winners (and wieners), each with their own demons, sharing a sausage bun with Michael Jordan, might he have finally got in with a good crowd? Possibly. There have been countless comebacks within this gang, and don't we all love one of those! Higgins may not remember going to the Caribbean, despite visiting twelve islands, but thanks to a life-long love affair with condensed milk, he does remember having something called a Guinness Punch.

Tipped off by Killy about the Guinness, the Hurricane has brought whole fat milk, cans of condensed milk, cinnamon, nutmeg, a bottle of dark rum, his cocktail shaker and bags of ice, all in a handy wheeled coolbox. Dispatching his Black Velvet, he knocks up a Guinness Punch and all is right with the world. He offers Fatima Whitbread a taste and she CANNOT BELIEVE how good it is. He whips one up for her and they sit together, sipping in the sun, lovely milky moustaches adorning their upper lips.

As Killy has revealed, the hot dog has it all for a nice day out and a picnic lunch.

Simply fill a Thermos with boiling water and pop the franks in before leaving the house, or once you've bought them from the shop. This way when your gang are ready for their hot dogs, so are you. You could grill them on the fender of your car, like they did in *Happy Days*, but I don't know how to do that!

The cheap buns you get in the shops are perfect for the task and last for ages. If you're lucky, you might even be able to buy Martin's Long Potato Rolls and be laughing all the way to the sausage bank. ('Laughing all the way to the bank' – Liberace coined that phrase.)

The problem with talking about toppings is that there are so many! Think about things you love, things you have left over from yesterday's dinner, and ask yourself: could I put that/would I want that, on a sausage? The variations are endless, which is the joy of the thing.

If you don't have a coolbox, try and wrap your cold drinks in something soft and ideally padded. A jumper, a towel, a gilet, even a knee support will all offer some form of insulation.

HACKS

Eight things to make old-fashioned picnics a bit better

1 A cool box: chock-full of ice and ice-cold beverages, anything fish-related and some real-glass glasses – EVEN KRUG TASTES CRAP OUT OF A PLASTIC GLASS!

2 A read of this silly book of mine: even though there's errant silliness, there are MANY GOLDEN IDEAS FOR AMAZING PICNICKING...

3 Fly swatter: for the inevitable flies and wasps.

4 A way of playing music for some considerable time.

5 A cold starter, a hot main course (use that Thermos!) and a proper pudding: treat it like a meal and control the menu like Julia Child would – add a sense of occasion and it will all be more fun, more delicious and more memorable.

6 Proper crockery and real cutlery ... and a bin bag.

7 Think about what you're going to cook over the few days beforehand: leftovers are one of the great picnic weapons.

8 Always, always, bring enough cigarettes, some spare lighters and that bloody kitbag (page 23).

Green Chilli – for the Perfect Hot Dog

Swear down, this is a sensational chilli recipe in its own right, regardless of the presence of a certain iconic sausage. In the UK, we are hardwired to think of chilli as a thick, rich, tomato-y chilli con carne type thing, but it doesn't have to be like that. This little beauty is herb-heavy and, as a result, the finished chilli is drier and more fragrant than you might expect. It's a spicy little number, too, which works well with a nice smoked frank in a bun, helped along with a zigzag of mustard and ketchup. Never mind the hot dog; it would be fantastic served with rice, a load of shredded spring onions, some sour cream, maybe a cheeky bit of guacamole and a big squeeze of lime. It's badass either way.

Makes enough for 8 dogs

2 tablespoons olive oil
500 g (1 lb 2 oz) minced (ground) pork – preferably nice and fatty, at least 10% fat content
1 teaspoon salt
1 onion, roughly chopped
2 garlic cloves, grated
2 green (bell) peppers, deseeded and roughly chopped
6 green chillies, finely sliced
1 teaspoon dried oregano
1 large handful of parsley, leaves picked and chopped
1 large handful of coriander (cilantro), leaves picked and chopped
1 large handful of mint, leaves picked and chopped
2 large tomatoes, chopped
2 tablespoons white wine vinegar
8 cooked hot dogs, to serve
8 potato rolls (page 54) or store-bought hot dog buns, to serve

Place a heavy-based saucepan over a high heat and add the olive oil. When it's nice and hot, add your pork and salt and roughhouse it with a wooden spoon. You want to press it against the pan and create a nice flat layer. Leave this for a full minute to crisp and brown, then roughhouse again, pressing the meat against the pan and leaving for another full minute. Do this once more, then it's time to start adding layers of flavour.

Add the onion, garlic, green peppers and chillies and stir into the meat. Keep the heat high, as you want the onions and veg to catch and char. Stir occasionally. When brown flecks start appearing on your veg, add the oregano and all the fresh herbs, stirring to combine. Next add the chopped tomatoes, including all the juice they've left behind on the board, then stir in the vinegar and bring to the boil.

Now you can reduce the heat to a very gentle simmer and cook the chilli for 30 minutes. The chilli will be quite dry, but you want that, so don't be alarmed. Give it a taste and adjust the seasoning, adding a little extra salt or vinegar to your preference. Allow to cool slightly and hot dog your way into the sunset.

Potato Rolls

Why not learn to make your own potato rolls, aka the perfect hot dog or burger bun. Please bear in mind that all bread is much easier made in a stand blender/ mixer thing than with your hands.

Makes 18 rolls

2½ teaspoons dried active yeast
50 g (2 oz/¼ cup) caster
  (superfine) sugar
750 ml (25 fl oz/3 cups) warm
  whole milk
500 g (1 lb 2 oz/4 cups) plain
  (all-purpose) flour

225 g (8 oz) leftover mashed potato
2 teaspoons salt
85 g (3 oz) butter, softened
2 large eggs, lightly beaten

For the egg wash
1 egg
1 tablespoon whole milk

Start by mixing the yeast and sugar into your warm milk. Let it stand for 5–10 minutes to get frothy and active.

Meanwhile, put your flour, mashed potato and salt into an electric mixer or a large bowl. Mix to combine, then make a well in the centre and add the butter, eggs and the yeast mixture. Using a dough hook or your hands, bring together and knead the dough briefly until it feels elastic and forms a smooth ball.

Place the dough in a lightly oiled bowl and cover with cling film (plastic wrap) or a tea towel. Leave in a warm, dark place until doubled in size, which should take around an hour.

Generously oil a high-sided baking tray (pan), roughly 38 cm x 24 cm x 7.5 cm (15 in x 10 in x 3 in). Knock back your dough with a firm punch or two, then remove from the bowl and shape into a nice thick log about 46 cm (18 in) long. Cut the log into 2.5 cm (1 in) pieces and roll into balls (if you're using them for burgers) or long rolls (if you're using them for hot dogs). Place on the baking tray so they are slightly spaced out, but close enough to touch each other as they rise and prove. Cover lightly and leave to rise again for 1 hour.

Preheat the oven to 180°C (350°F/gas 4).

Beat the egg and milk together for the egg wash, then brush over each roll. Bake the rolls for 25–30 minutes (you might want to rotate the baking tray after 15 minutes so they cook evenly), or until risen and lightly browned. When ready, remove from the oven and allow the rolls to cool on the tray for 15 minutes before transferring them to a wire rack.

Guinness Punch

One of the (many) things I treat myself to on a warm summer evening in Finsbury Park is a Guinness Punch from the Jamaican takeaway round the corner from my flat – it's a glorious drink, like a milkshake, especially if you go with the rum, too. Which I do, obviously. Hahhaha.

1 teaspoon nutmeg
1 teaspoon cinnamon
1 teaspoon vanilla extract
500ml (16 fl oz/2 cups) Bottled
  Guinness Foreign Extra Stout
  or Special Export

250ml (8 fl oz/1 cup) full fat
  (whole) milk
175ml (⅔ cup) condensed milk
A two-handed heap of ice cubes
A 50ml (¼ cup/2 fl oz) shot of
  dark rum

Put everything in the blender apart from the ice. Blend. Pour over the ice, put your feet up, close your eyes and say cheers to Jamaica for introducing you to the drink of the summer.

If I'm making them at home, I sometimes put a little Guinness float on top of my punch like in the photo on page 45 – just for the LOLs.

Black Velvet

Sweetings restaurant is a wonderful snapshot of the London of the 1890s. It is the restaurant Fergus Henderson based St John on, and where he proposed to his wife. For one of the archetypal London experiences, go for lunch at Sweetings. Start with a Black Velvet, and have a cold starter, then some fish, then a savoury, then pudding. Have a half pint of BV, though, not a full pint, as it gets a bit much. In her cookbook You're All Invited, Margot Henderson (wife of Fergus) describes the Black Velvet as:

'The perfect drink for a birthday breakfast. Best served in a pewter or silver tankard [as they do at Sweetings] if you have any, otherwise a half-pint glass [as they do at St John].

Pour in Champagne, about half to three-quarters full, and slowly top up with Guinness. Both can be poured into jugs beforehand and then into glasses as needed – this will cut down on the froth. It's also important to pour the Guinness last [and slowly], otherwise you get a massive amount of foam.'

A High Tea Picnic

Many relationships are made up of a flower and a gardener. The flower, outwardly at least, seems to dominate. The gardener, often under-appreciated, illuminates their partner, allowing their best qualities to shine through, while tempering their worst. Without a gardener tending to them, many flowers would be nothing but an ego shouting into a wind tunnel. Of course, there are also countless successful relationships between two gardeners and two flowers. Rather unflatteringly, I suspect the way this applies to me is that I think I am the flower, whereas in fact I am only *allowed* to think that by the one who really is …

This picnic is here to show how utterly delightful it is to celebrate the unsung: casting the familiar favourites as the stars of the show, instead of in the wings. To host, we have two friends, bonded in mutual understanding, since the sugar-and-spice fest that is this tea-party picnic is exclusively for others who are often maligned and frequently taken for granted. All the guests on this particular fantasy train have been instructed to bring along a little something to eat that is also often undervalued – but that, when looked at objectively, glistens like gold.

MENU

Spiced-up Sandwiches

Coconut Macaroons

Battenberg Cake

Cannoli

Ice Slushies

Fantasy Hosts
Debbie McGee and Ringo Starr

Fantasy Guests
Carmela Soprano, Piglet, Gromit, Mutley, Luigi

Location
In our heads, we are in the garden of the McGee abode, which is a bit like a Disney Castle, but on the banks of the River Thames in Oxfordshire. Any garden will do, though! Just get your mates round, have a good rummage in your cupboards, and tell everyone to bring something sweet, naughty and neglected that they remember from their childhood.

Dress Code
Whatever you like. This a not a day to have someone else tell you what to wear.

A High Tea Picnic

Unpacking the Hamper

DING-DONG!! In our fantasy picnic set-up, Debbie wakes up from her recurring dream, in which someone is plunging a sword deep into her side and realises the doorbell is ringing. OMG! It's only Ringo Starr!

'Ringo!' she shouts. 'What a treat, babe! It's been ages!'

Ringo's taken his spice rack with him everywhere since realising that cooking from Ottolenghi had left him with 600 jars of spices he'd only used once. Now he's 80, it also lets him crack the gag that these are the only powders he touches these days. Legend.

When the butler returns from the supermarket with a sarnie platter, Ringo grabs his rack and goes IN. He picks out a particularly sad egg mayo number, sprinkles curry powder in the sandwich and gives Debbie a taste.

'OMFG, it's like kedgeree!' she trills in excitement. 'That. Is. Amazing. Babes, you're a genius.' She asks Ringo what he'd put on her cheese sandwich.

He strokes his beard and remembers being on tour in Amsterdam: 'I was given a piece of Gouda, Debbie. Lovely bit of cheese – it had cumin seeds in it and it was delicious. So cumin, Debbie, I'd put cumin in it.' He's a natural!

Debbie has moved on to tuna and cucumber now and she's had the brilliant idea of adding some smoked paprika. Hands down though, French's mustard is her favourite condiment. She gives Ringo some to try.

'I love it,' he says, in his laid-back Scouse drawl. 'Do you know all it tastes of is turmeric, baby! Anything with ham, Debbie, anything toasted, and especially anything with cheese, try it with some turmeric. It'll blow your back doors off.' Debbie is overjoyed.

The first guest to arrive is the greatest of all the scene-stealers, Carmela Soprano, clutching a bottle of Vin Santo. She's got her Tupperware back from that bitch Janice and has filled it with biscotti – twice-baked – for dunking in the Vin Santo of course.

DING-DONG!! Piglet, Gromit and Mutley arrive next. Never ones to waste a day out, they've been paintballing and arrive high on adrenalin, running their mouths at a hundred miles an hour. 'We stopped off at the bakery in the village on the way,' Piglet says, frantically leaping with joy. 'I've got my old favourite, coconut macaroons, and Gromit's got a Battenberg. Mutley, what is it you've got?' Sniggering uncontrollably, Mutley is incomprehensible, so Piglet goes for a look. 'Oh gosh, yes,' he says, 'Mutley's got flapjacks.'

Last to arrive is Luigi; he's got a cute little lunchbox containing his mother's famous cannoli, filled with whipped ricotta spiked with shards of dark chocolate and candied peel.

'What's to drink?' I hear you cry. The obvious choice with this kind of tucker is tea, and of course Debbie has made a pot for those who insist. But she's keen to push the boat out a bit, too, and has persuaded a Hawaiian friend to bring his shaved ice cart over and let everyone go wild on her cupboard full of squashes and cordials. Crushed ice and sickly syrup – is there a greater treat?

Pack your own

Almost all the bounty for this picnic can be bought at fancy or not-so-fancy bakeries the world over. You're looking for delicious things that might appreciate a sprinkling of spice, or that will fill your mouth with cream. Independent high-street bakeries are often best for nostalgic treats and often at bargain prices. Otherwise, supermarkets now have most of this stuff, plus half-decent fresh cream eclairs, etc, in their fridges. As for the slushies, if you can't be arsed freezing and shaving a big block of ice with your kitchen grater, just toss a handful of ice cubes into a powerful blender – tread carefully, as some blenders struggle to cope with such heavy work – blitz to the texture of snow and then syrup it up. Pomegranate molasses is really good (the other day, I tried a mix of Ribena and pomegranate molasses that blew my tiny mind), and Rose's Lime Cordial is strong but good if that's your thing!

Coconut Macaroons

As I said, bakeries sell many excellent versions of all of all these sweet things, but making stuff is fun. Particularly redolent of Ben Benton's childhood, one of the hardest to find, and easiest to make, is the good old coconut macaroon. For the full effect, dip the bottoms of your cooled macaroons in melted chocolate and drizzle additional chocolate on top of them. They are delicious if you do, delicious if you don't – follow your heart and enjoy. Here's a failsafe recipe to make whenever you have a craving.

Makes about 20

400 g (14 oz) desiccated coconut
250 g (9 oz) condensed milk
2 large egg whites

¼ teaspoon salt
2 tablespoons melted dark chocolate,
    for drizzling (optional)

Preheat the oven to 160°C (320°F/gas 2) and line a baking tray (pan) with baking parchment.

Place the coconut and condensed milk in a large bowl and stir together until combined; the coconut should be moistened but not overly wet.

In another bowl, whisk the egg whites and salt together until they hold stiff peaks, then gently fold into the coconut mixture.

When completely combined, scoop out tablespoonfuls of the mix and gently roll into balls, then place on the prepared baking tray, giving each one a gentle press with the palm of your hand to flatten it slightly.

Bake the macaroons for 30 minutes or until lightly golden. Allow to cool on a wire rack for at least 30 minutes before drizzling with chocolate (optional) and eating (not optional).

Battenberg Cake

Gosh how good is Battenberg Cake?! It is fiddly to make though, as you can see from the lovely wonk in the one Ben made in the photo. If you're even a little baking-phobic, or easily annoyed, just buy one. If you do however, have the time, inclination and patience, you will be amply rewarded.

Makes 1 cake

150 g (5 oz) butter, at room temperature, plus extra to grease
150 g (5 oz/⅔ cup) caster (superfine) sugar
2 large free-range eggs

150 g (5 oz/1¼ cups) self-raising (self-rising) flour
2 drops red food colouring
3–4 tablespoons raspberry jam, for spreading
400 g (14 oz) shop-bought marzipan

Preheat the oven to 180°C (350°F/gas 4) and grease and line a small baking tray (pan), roughly 24 cm x 18 cm x 5 cm (9½ in x 7 in x 2 in). Using foil, create a firm barrier down the middle of the tray, to make sure the batters don't run into each other.

As with so many good classic cakes, you need to start by creaming together the butter and sugar until they are pale and fluffy, almost white. This is easiest done in a stand mixer or with a hand whisk and may take as long as 5 minutes. Next, mix in the eggs, one at a time, ensuring that the first one is fully incorporated before adding the next. Finally, ditch the whisk and, using a large metal spoon, gently fold in the flour.

Add half the cake mixture into one half of the baking tray. Now add the red food colouring to the other half of the mixture in the bowl and combine thoroughly, then carefully spoon this pink cake mixture into the other half of the baking tray.

Bake for 30 minutes or until a skewer inserted in the centre comes out clean. Remove the cakes from the oven and allow to cool in the tin for a couple of minutes before turning out onto a wire rack and leaving to cool fully.

Meanwhile, roll out your marzipan into a perfect square, roughly 30 cm x 30 cm (12 in x 12 in) and about 3 mm thick, then keep it covered with a clean tea towel.

Now all that's left to do is the assembly. Cut the two coloured sections of cake in half lengthways and trim the edges to give you four neat, similar-sized strips. Spread each strip of cake with raspberry jam on all sides and sandwich them together in alternating pairs. Lay the sandwiched cakes in the centre of your marzipan rectangle and roll the whole thing tightly. Finally, sit the cake on a board so the seam is underneath and trim off any excess. *Voila!*

Make some tea, slice a good chunk of Battenberg and sit back, smug as you like.

Nick Bramham's Amazing Ricotta-filled Cannoli

Nick Bramham (currently cooking at Quality Wines, next to my favourite restaurant in London, The Quality Chop House) makes the best cannoli I have ever eaten (and I've been to Sicily). There are recipes for cannoli that require less equipment, but these are SO GOOD, I just had to give you Nick's recipe. You'll need cannoli moulds, a (disposable) piping (pastry) bag, an 8 cm (3 in) pastry ring, a stand mixer and a pasta machine for these.

Makes 30 cannoli

200 g (7 oz) type '00' flour
1 tablespoon caster (superfine) sugar
1 generous tablespoon of lard (pork fat)
80 ml (3 fl oz) red wine
Rapeseed (canola) oil, for deep-frying

For the filling
500 g (1 lb 2 oz) ricotta (the best you can find)
75 g (2½ oz) icing (confectioner's) sugar
75 g (2½ oz) dark chocolate, chopped into shards
35 g (1¼ oz) candied peel, finely chopped

First, make the pastry. Combine all the dry ingredients in a stand mixer with a dough hook and combine. Add the lard and the wine and knead in the stand mixer for 5 minutes, until a smooth ball of dough has formed. Wrap the dough in cling film (plastic wrap) and leave it in the fridge for 30 minutes to relax.

For the filling, combine the ricotta and icing sugar in a large bowl and beat to combine, then stir in the chocolate and peel. Chill in the fridge until needed.

Roll the dough through the pasta machine going down one notch at a time until you reach the thinnest setting. Cut the dough sheet into circles with the pastry ring and wrap round the moulds sealing the join with egg white. Using your fingers, make sure the ends are dramatically sloped and the dough is an even thickness.

To fry the cannoli, turn on your deep-fryer or pour oil into a heavy-based saucepan until it is two-thirds full then heat it to 190°C (370°F). Roll each pastry disc around a cannoli mould, sealing the end with a little water and a good press of your finger. Once you have rolled six or so, carefully drop slip them into the hot oil, mould and all, and fry for 1–2 minutes, until they are golden brown and just starting to blister. Drain on paper towels and allow to cool slightly.

Using tongs, carefully slip the cannoli off their moulds, then roll and fry the next batch. Repeat until all the cannoli are cooked.

To fill, spoon your filling into a piping bag with quite a wide nozzle. Start at one end of each cannoli and pipe from the centre out to the edge, then do the same at the other end. All you need to do now is *mangare*!

HACKS

Six things to do with a drink from a fast-food outlet – go on, plan ahead, try stuff out and stash some miniatures in your coat pockets.

1
Add Campari
to a Fanta.

2
Add red wine
to a Coca-Cola.

3
Add hot coffee
to a milkshake or McFlurry.

4
Add Baileys, brandy
or Fernet-Branca
to a black coffee.

5
Add whiskey (and coffee?)
to a chocolate
(or vanilla) milkshake.

6
Add white wine
to a lemonade.

A Picnic Can Chan

e the World

Few artists change the way a landscape looks, and even fewer change how we look at everything. But Little Richard and Picasso did both, and that's why they've buddied up with this motley crew today – all of them have changed the landscape.

Born in Macon, Georgia, in 1932, Richard Wayne Penniman was beaten by his father from a young age for wearing his mother's clothes and makeup, and ended up being thrown out of the house when he was fifteen. Resilient and flamboyant, Little Richard would become a natural performer, and with 'Tutti-Frutti', 'Long Tall Sally' and 'Lucille' already under his belt by 1957, he was off like a firework, busy (along with a few others) inventing rock 'n' roll. His massive hair, glitzy outfits and lavish makeup were legendary, as was the frantic energy of his live shows – it was as if someone had plugged him into the mains. In one live recording he SCREAMED at the crowd, 'I'm Little Richard, the most beautiful man in music, and wherever you're going, I'm already back.' The room went wild.

From one enormous talent to another. Our other Fantasy Host is a man in possession of artistic talents so broad and diverse that he is impossible to categorise. Pablo Picasso may not have done much for twentieth-century dress sense, but his influence encompassed almost everything else. The intensity and sheer genius of the man when you watch him paint on film is mind-blowing. In *A Visit to Picasso* (1949), we see him paint a blade of grass with one brush stroke, turn it into an ox with a second and into a woman with a third – an illusion so complete, a trick so artful, that even the late, great Paul Daniels wouldn't have known what to do with himself. Picasso's ability to work across mediums, to express himself and reveal the world to us in so many different ways, makes him, for me, the most diverse and talented artist ever to have lived.

And so to the chosen picnic of these two game-changers: roast chicken. Why? Because the landscape of picnicking needs to be transformed, and chicken might just be the foodstuff to do it.

Poached Chicken

Chicken-stuffed Pumpkin

Chicken Liver Pâté of Dreams

Gribenes with Schmaltz Mayo

Kalimotxo

Fantasy Hosts
Little Richard and Picasso

Fantasy Guests
Yayoi Kusama, Andy Goldsworthy, Alexander Calder, Felice Varini, Camille Walala

Location
An urban wasteland. Do you need an idyllic setting for a truly memorable al fresco meal or can you bring the party yourself? With trompe-l'oeil master, and one of my favourite artists of all time, Felice Varini and the glorious Camille Walala about, there is certainly hope for the latter. (Have a Google of what Walala has recently done to a not particularly beautiful street in Leyton, London.)

The answer of course, is that beauty can be found, and installed, literally anywhere – and so can an excellent picnic.

Dress Code
Smart casual – a happy medium for everyone.

Unpacking the Hamper

Little Richard, very sensibly , asks Picasso why, of all the places they could be, they are in this grim car park behind a provincial cinema? Picasso explains that if only he'd read the emails, he'd know that everyone coming today looks at things that are seemingly bland and innocuous and turns them into gold.

Despite a reputation that might suggest otherwise, Picasso isn't much of a gourmand. He has maintained a relatively puritanical approach to food throughout his life. His two favourite things to eat are eel stew and an omelette tortilla Niçoise. Today, though, he has broken rank and told the gang to riff on roast chicken.

Little Richard has riffed so much that he's poached his chicken not roasted it. He tells them he usually cannot cook for toffee, but his poached chicken is so good because he's got the best method EVER. 'It works no matter the size of the bird. You bring a massive pan of well-salted water to the boil with plenty of veg, like leeks and carrots and garlic, some spices and some vinegar and anything else you fancy. Then you put the chicken in so it is completely submerged. Bring it back to the boil, skim off any scum, put the lid on the pot, turn off the heat and leave it alone for 90 minutes. That's it. Every time, without fail, perfect poached chicken and a wonderful broth to guzzle down later.'

Little Richard's on a culinary roll. 'The best thing about poached chicken,' he says, 'is the skin. It's so soft you can take it off the bird in big strips and fry it slowly for a real long time. They go so crunchy it's mad and they're called gribenes! Loads of fat (schmaltz) comes out, which you can then mix into mayo with some salt and malt vinegar, like this.' He's banging some of everything into a baguette: poached chicken, gribenes, schmaltz mayo and some lettuce. Shake, shake, shake with some hot sauce, a squeeze of lemon and he's off.

Picasso, simple as one of his beloved goats, has just stuffed a whole head of garlic cloves (split up) into his chicken and roasted it. He rips big strips of meat from his bird, dunks them in Little Richard's mayo and lays them in his baguette. He then squeezes the oozy roast garlic cloves out of their skin into the sandwich. Pleasingly Provençal.

What with her lifelong love of both the polka dot and the pumpkin, Yayoi Kusama wasn't gonna let Picasso and his 'just a chicken' email get in the way of her knocking out something rather spectacular.

Having lit a fire and tended it a while, she sits a whole pumpkin on a large, flat stone and manoeuvres the lot into the middle of the fire. The flames begin to lick around the pumpkin and the smell is sweet and wonderful. Little Richard is incensed on Picasso's behalf. He reminds Yayoi that the agreement was to bring a chicken, not a pumpkin. But she explains that she wants this pumpkin to echo the truths the universe might hold, like one of her extraordinary *Infinity Rooms*.

After a few hours, Kusama's pumpkin, black and shrivelling, is plucked from the fire. Cutting it in half, she reveals a whole deboned chicken, steamed to perfection inside the malty caramelised pumpkin. Kusama is pleased and Andy Goldsworthy has turned up late with some chicken liver pâté inside a mini version of one of his famous black rocks.

As the rest of the gang settle down to eat, Andy is busy meticulously picking the meat from the bones of Picasso's chicken. Combining the bones with some from his pocket, he arranges them all in concentric circles on the ground. Kusama observes that it is so enticing that it might lead you through the circle to the centre of the earth.

Alexander Calder, Felice Varini and Camille Walala are setting up the bar. They've spent hours adorning the site with multicoloured paint and tape, and Calder has fashioned a tiny tinkling mobile from bits of rubbish and chicken bones he's found lying around – hanging from the top of the bar, its arms are like delicate branches, leaves rippling in the breeze.

Picasso has been very specific: he will drink wine – white, pink or red – and nothing else. Varini, always keen to play with perception, decides that every drink will be wine-based, but not be wine itself. Little Richard is keen to get his drink on and go for a walk, and he likes Varini's idea. 'What's that one the Spanish have?' Varini's on it: 'Sangria?' 'Nope.' Little Richard is thinking. 'Red wine and coke?'

he ventures. '*Kalimotxo*' Varini weighs in, 'red wine and coke. People are so sniffy about it, but it's a great beverage for a (car)park picnic! And you can get away with having it without ice. Just.' What a night!

Pack your own

Those little rotisserie chickens most supermarkets sell are one of the greatest gifts to picnicking. Failing that, buy some cooked chicken drummers and gnaw away to your heart's content. With some chicken, a lemon, a lettuce, a baguette and a pot of mayonnaise, you're in seventh bloody heaven in the park or at your desk. If you want to try something truly spectacular, have a go at Kusama's chicken stuffed inside a pumpkin – it's wonderful how the malty pumpkin takes on the flavour of the chicken, and the chicken stays pure and delicate. The whole thing is surprisingly good cold too, like a slice of terrine, squeezed with lemon and seasoned up.

Chicken-stuffed Pumpkin

The skill here lies in the deboning of the chicken: you can ask your trusty butcher to do it for you (good luck!), or you can watch a YouTube video and practise at home. It isn't impossible, but you do need a small, sharp knife and to be quite deft with it. You don't need to cook this stuffed pumpkin over an open fire like Kusama did, but you do need to cook it. This is a portable sensation bar none.

Serves 8–10

1 x 1.5–2 kg (3 lb 7 oz–4 lb 7 oz) whole organic chicken, deboned
1 large pumpkin (squash)
1 tablespoon salt

1 tablespoon freshly ground black pepper
75 g (2½ oz) butter
Juice of 1 lemon

Preheat the oven to 250°C (500°F/gas 9), or as hot as it will go.

Start by cutting off the top of the pumpkin, keeping the little 'hat' to go on top again afterwards. Scoop out all the seeds and hollow out a little of the pumpkin flesh – just enough to make room for the chicken to fit inside.

Lay out the deboned chicken on a board and season liberally with salt and pepper. Season the inside of the pumpkin, too.

Now fold the chicken so that the thigh and wing meat is enveloped around the breast meat, then push the folded chicken inside the pumpkin. Spread the butter on top of the chicken. Sit the 'hat' back on top of the pumpkin – you can tie it on with kitchen twine, or secure it with toothpicks (both wetted so they don't catch light during the cooking), if you like – but just balancing it on top should be more than fine.

Put the pumpkin in a roasting tin and pour in 250 ml (8½ fl oz/1 cup) water. Place on the middle shelf of the oven, then immediately reduce the temperature to 170°C (340°F/gas 3). Cook the stuffed pumpkin for about 2 hours or until a skewer inserted into the centre comes out cleanly and has enough heat in it to make you wince when it is pressed to your lip – or you can opt for the less alarming method of checking the chicken has reached an internal temperature of 75°C/165°F. When it's ready, take the pumpkin out of the oven and let it sit for half an hour before serving.

This is delicious served in messy wedges with a sprinkle of salt, a squeeze of lemon and a green salad. It also makes quite a spectacular sight when cut into at a picnic.

Chicken Liver Pâté of Dreams

This is for those wonderful moments when you splash out on a posh chicken and find a little baggy of plum-coloured organs inside its cavity – you normally get just enough chicken liver for a little portion of pâté. Of course, you can also buy chicken livers separately – then you can make pâté to your heart's content.

Makes enough for 6–8 servings on toast

100 g (4 oz) cold unsalted butter
1 small red onion (or half a larger one),
   very finely diced
1 garlic clove, grated
½ teaspoon salt

2 tablespoons brandy
200 g (7 oz) chicken livers removed
   from the milk and dried,
   sinewy bits removed
6 grinds of black pepper

This one moves fast, so have all your ingredients weighed out and ready before embarking on the cooking.

Melt 30 g (1 oz) of the butter in a non-stick frying pan (skillet) over a medium-high flame. When it is frothing, add the onion and garlic and ¼ teaspoon of the salt and fry quite hard in the foaming butter for 2 minutes, or until soft and just starting to brown. Standing well back add the brandy to the pan – it may well flame, which is exciting.

Let the flame subside and reset yourself.

Dump the contents of the pan into the blender.

Increase the heat to high and add another 30 g (1 oz) of butter. When it is foaming, spread out the livers in the pan and cook for a full minute, turn over and cook again for a full minute so they are seared brown, with a little crust. Add the remaining ¼ teaspoon of salt and the pepper, tossing quickly to coat.

Tip the livers into the food processor, with the last 40 g (1½ oz) of butter and blend to a perfectly smooth paste. Test for seasoning, it might well need some more salt. Pass through a sieve with a wooden spoon, into an appropriate, receptacle and allow to cool.

If you want to eat it now, go for it, but if you want to keep it for later, melt a little more butter in a clean pan and pour over the top of the pâté covering it completely, then refrigerate it – this will create an airtight seal, preserving the pâté for a week or so.

Gribenes with Schmaltz Mayo

For the unacquainted few, gribenes is the name given to skin left behind when chicken fat, or schmaltz, is rendered; mixed with fried onions, it becomes wonderfully crisp and chewy.

We're making a decent amount of schmaltz here, about 250 g (9 oz). You only need a few tablespoons for the mayo, but you can freeze the rest in portions, ready to use whenever you get a craving. If you're anything like me, you'll soon be spreading schmaltz mayo on everything and anything, and dunking stuff in it, too.

Makes enough for a crowd

500 g (1 lb 2 oz) chicken skin
250 ml (8 fl oz/1 cup) water
1 small onion, roughly diced

Salt
2–3 tablespoons store-bought mayo
A dash of white wine vinegar

Start by chopping the skin and fat into nice thin, long strips – it is much easier to do this with cold chicken skin, so fridge or freeze it first and use your sharpest knife.

Place the skin/fat in a heavy-based saucepan with the water and bring to a simmer over a medium–high heat, then turn the heat down to a low simmer and cook slowly for at least 1½ hours. You want to take your time with this: give it a stir occasionally to stop anything sticking, but otherwise leave it to do its thing. Over time all the water will evaporate, the chicken skin will turn golden brown and there'll be loads of fat in the pan. This fat is liquid gold. Add the onion and keep cooking and stirring now and again until the skin and onion are both well browned.

Remove from the heat and carefully strain the contents of the pan into a heatproof bowl through as fine a sieve as you can muster. You now have a bowl of schmaltz.

Tip the gribenes out of the sieve on to a paper-towel-lined tray or large plate, sprinkle with a little salt and leave to cool. Open a beer. Drink some and eat some. Depending how many tablespoons of schmaltz you reckon you have, you want that many tablespoons of mayo.

Put the mayo in a bowl, with a sploosh of vinegar to offset the fatty schmaltz. Tip the schmaltz in and start to stir slowly. It will look dodgy. at first, but soon your mayo will all come back together. Check if it needs a pinch of salt to be even more delicious. Keep drinking that beer.

Start dunking gribenes in the mayo and drinking your beer. Right now, wherever you are, you are one of the naughtiest people in your vicinity. Serve them to your friends or keep them for yourself. The more you eat, the thirstier you will be. What a wonderful position to be in. As long as you have enough beers …

HACKS

Six great ways to eat one of the great gifts to picnicking – the supermarket rotisserie chicken

1. Make coleslaw, chicken and hot sauce sandwiches.

2. Make chicken, iceberg lettuce, mayo, Tabasco and lemon juice sandwiches.

3. Shred all the meat down, and mix it with yoghurt, mayonnaise and loads of curry powder for one of the most delicious things in the world.

4. Buy ready-made sandwiches (or anything) and load them up with chicken.

5. Add the meat to a Thermos of instant noodles, pasta, broth or pretty much anything – it's chicken, innit?

6. Eat the chicken, unadorned, like Henry VIII – they're SO GOOD.

A Scone-based Pic

ic

Treat 'em mean, keep 'em keen, sounds like time for scones and cream.

In this book of completely made-up relationships between people who either have not, or could not, have ever met, Snoop and Martha stand alone as great friends in real life. On their various TV appearances together (and their show *Martha and Snoop's Potluck Dinner Party*), their admiration for and enjoyment of each other is palpable, indeed wonderful to behold.

Their first encounter, as two strangers on a TV 'roasting' of Justin Bieber, saw Snoop fall head over heels for Martha. He has since described their meeting as 'Holy matrimony and holy macaroni all at the same time.'

Until 1802, it was thought that clouds were unique and therefore unclassifiable. That year a professional chemist and amateur meteorologist called Luke Howard, presented an essay to the Askesian Society detailing his findings about the clouds and other elements of our weather system. He pointed out that there were in fact three distinct types of cloud, and gave them the names we still use today: *cumulus* (meaning 'heap' in Latin), *stratus* ('layer') and *cirrus* ('curl of hair').

Ian Neale, of Newport, Wales, is a champion giant vegetable grower. His veg is so big that if you dropped it like it's hot, you'd break both your legs. At the time of publication, he holds the Guinness World Record for heaviest aubergine (eggplant), largest pepper (capsicum) and heaviest swede – the last an astonishing 54 kilos (close to 120 lb).

Somehow, Ian's prowess caught Snoop's attention and before playing a gig in Cardiff in 2011, he posted a video on his YouTube channel addressing 'my homeboy Ian Neale' directly, offering him tickets to the gig and explaining, 'I do vegetation myself, and I wanna know your secret.'

Subsequently interviewed on Sky News, Ian talks about having a smoke with Snoop: 'I don't normally smoke, you see, but he offered me one, so I took it.' 'I'm hoping that's just tobacco,' the journalist deadpans. 'No, it wasn't,' Ian says, giggling like a schoolgirl.

I was lucky enough to interview Ian Neale later that year for a BBC radio show. Standing next to his record-breaking swede, and wearing the same shirt he met Snoop in, I asked him if his swede had a name – Bjorn or something? 'No,' he replied sternly, adding 'I wouldn't want to upset it.' Then, in a moment of pure radio gold, he turned back to me and said, 'Although, now you mention it, I do have a turnip called Lucy.'

Snoop spends a lot of his time in a cloud and has met Ian Neale, Ian Neale could be said to have his head in the clouds, Martha loves a cloud of whipped cream and Luke Howard named the clouds. As far as I am concerned, THAT IS A REASON TO PICNIC.

MENU

Scones

Candied Marrow and Fennel Jam

Pumpkin and Ginger Jam

Homemade Clotted Cream

Assorted Teas

Fantasy Host
Snoop Dogg

Fantasy Guests
Martha Stewart, Ian Neale and Luke Howard

Location
Newport reservoirs, picnicking out the back of Ian Neale's Vauxhall Meriva.

Dress Code
I hope that you have looked up the Ian Neale/Snoop videos and seen Ian's amazing vegetable-medley shirt! I am going to run with the idea that Luke Howard has picked everyone outfits to wear: Snoop has lucked out and got a shirt with an enormous picture of Ian holding an enormous turnip; Martha has an enormous picture of Ian holding an enormous meringue and Luke Howard has cumulonimbus on his shirt.

Unpacking the Hamper

The gang is headed to Ian's favourite leafy spot up by the reservoirs outside Newport, South Wales. It's quite a place. While Ian tells Snoop all the secrets for fleecing your marrows to achieve maximum size without losing structure or firmness, Snoop takes notes. Not to be outdone by Ian's prowess, Snoop regales the guys with the story of when he set a world record himself, for making the world's largest Gin and Juice, at the BottleRock Napa Valley music festival in 2018. The beverage contained 180 bottles of gin, 156 bottles of apricot brandy and 106 litres (28 gallons) of orange juice.

Martha has made a batch of traditional scones. That's how she likes things done: properly. For a bit of jazz, she's brought three cream options: clotted cream, mascarpone and crème fraîche. I like to think that Martha is aware of a nifty whipped cream technique, whereby you put some double (heavy) cream in a jam jar with a bit of icing sugar, put the lid on tightly and keep shaking until your hands nearly drop off.

Ian has brought jams made from leftover bits of giant vegetables made by a friend. Everyone looks aghast at the idea of vegetable jams until Ian whips out some spoons gives everyone a try. The first is candied marrow and fennel. I imagine Snoop describing as 'Angel's Jelly' and the other is pumpkin and ginger, which Luke Howard refers to cryptically as 'Lucifer's Marmalade'.

Luke is in charge of the drinks today and as befits his nature, he is obsessed with tea. The chemist in him is intrigued by the alchemy of a simple cup. What, he can oft be found lonely wondering, is it that makes a perfect brew?

He has discovered three things: first, one teaspoon of loose leaf tea per 200 ml (7 fl oz) of water is about right; second, brewing tea for three minutes in freshly boiled water before pouring is rarely the wrong thing to do; and finally, it is the terroir of the tea that most affects its flavour. Luke has tried teas from India, Africa, Sri Lanka, China, Japan and Cornwall, all from the same plant, but they all taste so different!! 'It's like bloody wine!!' he has been heard shouting from the windows of 7 Bruce Grove, Tottenham, London, in 1852.

Luke asks each guest how they take their tea. Martha likes hers light and floral, without milk. He brews her a first-flush Darjeeling. Ian is very specific: he's a Barry's man, thank you, two bags to a cup, milk and two sugars. Luke goes for an Assam, over-brewing it by a minute or so, then adds a teaspoon of condensed milk to the Thermos and waits for the fireworks. Snoop, to be honest, isn't mad into tea and asks if Luke could do him something a little different. Unphased, Luke brews a tea from Yunnan with malty notes and a slight smokiness, then pours it into a Thermos half-full of ice and shakes well before pouring into a glass. Snoop is unsure at first, but the malty, chocolatey taste blows his mind.

Luke, for his sins, likes a rare Keemun Mao Feng, and he's keeping it to himself.

Pack your own

Most of the picnics in this book are encouraging of some innovation, but in this instance, we'll leave things alone. Unusually these days, the British seem to have this one right: scones, clotted cream and your favourite jam, all washed down with a nice cup of tea, is about as perfect as life gets.

If you can't be arsed to make clotted cream, jam or scones, fret not – we can't all be Martha Stewart or Ian Neale. Every store sells scones and jam, and often clotted cream as well. If you find yourself in a clotted-cream-less place, mascarpone, thick crème fraiche are still your friends. *Bon appetit.*

HACKS

Eight traditional picnic essentials pondered

1 **TUPPERWARE:**
unbelievably useful.

2 **WICKER BASKET:**
Complete nonsense!
Cumbersome clap-trap!
What's wrong with a
tote bag? A basket makes
pompous people feel posh
and tricks the rest of us
into thinking the crap
that came in it was worth
the money.

3 **PAPER PLATES:**
real crockery is better, but
good-quality plastic plates
are the best all-rounders.

4 **PAPER CUPS:**
good for mixing things
in, not great for drinking
out of – this is a picnic,
not a six-year-old's
birthday party.

5 **DISPOSABLE CUTLERY:**
go to the charity (thrift)
shop and buy some nice
old stuff instead.

6 **RUG:**
very nice, especially
those jazzy ones with
a waterproof layer
underneath.

7 **THERMOS:**
a miracle of modern
science and a total gift
to the picnicker – buy as
many as you can afford/
seems sensible.

8 **ICE PACKS:**
is it just me, or is there
something creepy about
ice packs? They're a lovely
idea, but a good-quality
cool box loaded up with
a bag or two of ice for
your Pimm's is a much
better one.

Perfect Scones

This is a belter of a recipe and now thrice stolen. Nigella nicked it off someone called Lily, Lily no doubt nicked it off someone else and Ben Benton has taken inspiration from Nigella as it makes him look really good. As Nigella says, if you like, you can add extra ingredients to the dough before you turn it out on to the worktop and roll it out. For this quantity you'll want about 75 g (2½ oz) of the extra ingredient if it is something like raisins or sultanas, or mature Cheddar, Gruyere or something.

Makes 12

500 g (1 lb 2 oz/4 cups) plain
   (all-purpose) flour
½ teaspoon salt
1 ½ teaspoons bicarbonate of soda
   (baking soda)

4½ teaspoons cream of tartar
75 g (2½ oz) cold unsalted butter, diced
300 ml (10 fl oz/1¼ cups) whole milk
1 large egg, beaten

Preheat the oven to 220°C (430°F/gas 8) and lightly grease a baking tray (pan).

Sift the flour, salt, bicarb and cream of tartar into a large bowl. Rub in the butter with your fingertips until it is fully incorporated. Add the milk and mix until the dough has just come together – do not overwork. Turn it out onto a floured surface and shape into a round. The dough should be a little raggedy, you are not after smooth perfection. This will help to keep the scones 'short', or light and fluffy to you and me.

Roll out the dough to a thickness of about 3 cm (1¼ in) thickness. Dip a cookie-cutter into some flour, then stamp out as many scones as you can from the first roll. You may need to re-roll to get the last few scones from the dough, but be careful to not over work.

Place the scones on the baking tray very close together, then brush the tops with the beaten egg. Bake for 10 minutes or until risen and golden.

Allow to cool a touch then break them in half and cover them in clotted cream and your favourite jam – bam thank you ma'am!

Candied Marrow and Fennel Jam

If, like Ian Neale, you are trying to grow some of the biggest vegetables on the planet, you'll need recipes like this for using up veg. If you just wanna make some unexpectedly delicious jam, buy a courgette (zucchini) or two and make this all the same. Despite its less than appealing sound, this is genuinely one of the most delicious jams you will ever swipe across a buttered/clotted creamed carb.

Makes enough for 2 x 500 ml (17 fl oz) jars

400 g (14 oz) marrow or courgettes (zucchini), peeled and cut into chunks
100 g (3½ oz) fennel, cut into small chunks

500 g (1 lb 2 oz) caster (superfine) sugar
2.5 cm (1 in) fresh root ginger, peeled and finely grated
1 lemon, juiced

You'll need a large saucepan for this. Start by putting your marrow and fennel into said pot and adding the caster sugar. Mix well so the sugar coats everything, then cover and leave to stand in a cool place for at least 2–3 hours, preferably overnight.

After the allotted time, put a small plate in the freezer (you'll need this to test for setting point later). Place the pot over a medium heat and warm gently, stirring occasionally, until the sugar has dissolved. Once it comes to the boil, add the ginger and lemon juice, reduce the heat to a nice steady simmer and cook until the cubes of marrow and fennel look transparent, about 20 minutes.

At this juncture, you will want to test whether the jam has reached setting point. To do this, take your plate from the freezer and carefully drop a teaspoonful of the jam on to it. If setting point has been reached, the jam should quickly form a skin, and if you push it gently with your finger it should crinkle up slightly. If not, continue to boil until setting point is reached, testing every 5–10 minutes or so.

Pour the jam into hot, sterilised jam jars and put the lids on at once. Leave to cool, then store in a cool dry place for up to 6 months. Once opened, keep in the fridge and eat within 2 weeks. This is mad delicious on toast with mascarpone as well as on Lily's/Nigella's/Ben's scones.

Pumpkin and Ginger Jam

The devil's confiture – this is a really perky jam. Texturally it is a little left-field, but the flavour is a pure sensation, and it really brings alive a scone or a crumpet or something. Whilst being an unashamedly sweet jam, it doubles up as a devilishly good chutney with cheese or even boiled meats. If you are going down that route, don't rule out adding a fresh red chilli at the beginning of the process.

Makes enough for 2 x 500 ml (17 fl oz) jars

600 g (1 lb 5 oz) pumpkin, peeled, deseeded and chopped into small chunks
500 g (1 lb 2 oz) caster (superfine) sugar

1 lemon, cut into wedges, pips removed
100 g (3½ oz) fresh root ginger, peeled and cut into rounds

Place the pan over a medium heat and bring to the boil. Meanwhile, blitz your lemon and ginger in a blender.

Once your jam comes up to the boil, add the ginger and lemon to the pan, reduce the heat to a gentle simmer and cook for 25–30 minutes. The pumpkin should be nice and soft by this point, so much so that you can mash it with a fork to a smooth-ish paste. If not, give it a little more time – you can't say fairer than that. When it is soft, mash the pumpkin with a fork or a stick blender.

Finally, all that is left to do is to pour the jam into hot, sterilised jam jars and cover at once. Leave to cool, then store in a cool dry place for up to 6 months; once opened, keep in the fridge and eat within 2 weeks.

Homemade Clotted Cream

This is a simple recipe for such a decadent result. As it takes 12 hours to do its stuff, why not pop it in the oven before you go to bed and have a warm vat of clotted cream ready for you in the morning?

Makes 1 litre (34 fl oz/4 cups)

1 litre (34 fl oz/4 cups) double (heavy) cream

Preheat the oven to 90°C (200°F/gas ¼).

Pour the cream into a shallow baking dish and bake it, uncovered, for 12 hours. You do not need to do anything: do not stir it, do not look at it, do not even think about it.

When the time is up, carefully remove from the oven and leave to cool at room temperature.

You'll end up with a thick layer of clotted cream, and possibly some thin cream beneath. You can spoon some from the top for eating right away. To keep the rest for future use, spoon the top layer of thick cream into a Kilner (Mason) jar or airtight container and chill in the fridge – it will last for up to 5 days. Any thin cream left in the dish can be kept in the fridge for a few days and used in cooking, baking, or added to your coffee or cereal.

A Rethinking of

A breakfast picnic is the very definition of intimacy.

the Picnic

Much-missed Anthony Bourdain once said there was nothing nicer you could do for someone than make them breakfast and I am inclined to agree. We are exposed at breakfast, it is very intimate. Stood there in our jimjams, asking someone how they like their eggs in the morning and if they'd like sugar in their coffee is often the beginning of a beautiful friendship.

As well as its potential romance, breakfast is also a great panacea. Sometimes I wake up all at sea and find myself pacing my flat insecure and panicky, I know what to do to calm myself down though, I reach for my favourite socks and lucky duck pants (seriously), get dressed and head for the 'greasy spoon' – a traditional British caff.

If what Bourdain says is true, the nicest man I have ever met is Mustafa from the Angel Café on Stroud Green Road in Finsbury Park. He's not my usual type admittedly, but I am pulled back from the brink somehow with a wink from him, a few of his inexplicably deep-fried sausages, some bacon, hash browns, a fried egg, two strong milky teas and a newspaper I wouldn't normally read.

This picnic is dedicated to three people who really needed someone nice to make them breakfast.

MENU

Full English Breakfast Shooter's Sandwich

Alan Turing's Crumpets

Breakfast Martini

Fantasy Host
Amy Winehouse

Fantasy Guests
Alan Turing, Donny Hathaway

Location
**The beach in Miami, near the recording studio
where Amy laid down tracks for both *Frank*
and *Back to Black*.**

Dress Code
**Comfy linen beach wear and a nice straw hat.
And the usual brown suit and tie for Alan, thank you.**

Unpacking the Hamper

Alan Turing is just lovely; he's like a character from Winnie the Pooh. On his lap are his hands, in his hands is his lunchbox, in his lunchbox is a tea towel, swaddled inside the tea towel are his crumpets. Inside his crumpets are flour, yeast, milk, bicarbonate of soda, salt and sugar.

All he needs is someone to toast them for him so he gets up, and heads to the kitchen to ask if they might do it. Alan hasn't only brought crumpets, he's got Marmite, marmalade and proper butter with him too. As he says, 'the butter in America is largely abominable. It's Irish Kerrygold or nothing for me.'

The gang are hiding from the sun outside their favourite beach bar and restaurant. Amy grabs Alan's marmalade heads behind the bar to mix them all 'a quick sharpener.'

Returning to the table with three sparkling breakfast martinis, she sits down and Alan's crumpets arrive. Being American, Donny has never had a crumpet.

'Get ready to have your mind blown,' Winehouse says.

The idea of a crumpet blowing Donny Hathaway's mind begins to look unlikely when he slams an enormous full English breakfast shooter's sandwich down on the table and begins carving it up like a cake.

Originally a way to make a beef Wellington portable, the shooter's sandwich is a round crusty loaf, top removed, hollowed out and slathered with pâté. It is then filled with layers of cooked steak, mustard and mushrooms. The lid is put back on and the whole thing is wrapped in baking parchment and pressed under a weight overnight. By the morning, it sets like a terrine and can be sliced into wedges.

Donny's doesn't have steak in it. He's filled his with a full English breakfast and is rightly rather pleased. Alan is certain that filling a loaf of bread with a fry-up and pressing it overnight is the best idea anyone has had since he invented the computer.

Inspired by Donny's sandwich, Alan suggests filling a Shooter with pancakes, bacon, maple syrup, pomegranate molasses, ricotta and blueberries. A silence descends, everyone sips their bejewelled beverage and appreciates how wonderful it is to be in the presence of genius.

Overcome with emotion, Amy tells Donny that not only is he her favourite recording artist of all time (which he was) but that *Live!* is the best live album ever recorded; Donny glows. Amy asks Alan who his favourite artist is and he eyes her quizzically, wondering how she couldn't already know ... Looking her dead in the eye, he tells her 'Well, Rembrandt, of course.'

Pack your own

A big batch of Breakfast Martinis could definitely be made in advance and popped in a Thermos to be drunk on the train with your breakfast but there's no shortcuts on the sandwich front I'm afraid. You are going to have to plan this in advance - there's just no way to rush a Shooter. It really is worth it though, I mean COME ON! A fry up you can put in your pocket!!

To carry your crumpets, wrap them in a tea towel, a hand towel, a bath towel or five or six handkerchiefs, the minute they are out of the toaster. If this warm bundle is packed in a rucksack straight away and only unwrapped when you are ready to eat, you should have enough warmth in the crump to still melt your butter when applied to its surface.

Full English Breakfast Shooter's Sandwich

Be warned: this one is a waiting game, but the reward is worth the wait.

Makes enough for 4 hungry breakfasters

12 rashers smoked streaky bacon
8 pork sausages
8 hash browns
Rapeseed (canola) oil we need,
  for frying
400 g (14 oz) mushrooms, finely sliced
1 garlic clove, grated

1 teaspoon salt
Juice of ½ lemon
1 medium round crusty loaf
6 free-range eggs
2 large beefheart tomatoes, sliced
  into rounds
Relish or ketchup, to serve (optional)

Preheat your oven to 220°C (430°F/gas 8) and line a couple of trays with foil.

Lay out the bacon, sausages and hash browns on the baking trays, then cook in the oven for 10 minutes. Check the bacon and turn it if needs be. Return the trays to the oven and keep cooking until the bacon is nice and brown and starting to crisp, about 5 minutes, then remove and set aside on a plate. Turn the sausages and hash browns and keep cooking for a further 10 minutes until golden brown and delicious.

Heat a frying pan until it is smoking hot, then pour in the oil. Add the mushrooms, settling them into a single layer and leaving them alone for a minute to get some colour. Toss them and then push into a single layer again and leave for a full minute to get more colour. Keep doing this until the mushrooms are browning nicely. At this point, add the garlic and salt and toss. As soon as you can smell garlic, remove the pan from the heat and add the lemon juice. Leave to one side to cool.

Cut the top off your loaf, about 2.5 cm (1 in) below the top. Using a small knife, or your fists, remove most of the inside of the loaf. Now start to build up your layers in your hollowed-out loaf: go your own way, but mushrooms is a nice place to start, perhaps followed by bacon, then hash browns, sausages, tomatoes and eggs. Push the layers down and place the lid on.

Tear off a couple of large sheets of baking parchment and a couple of even larger sheets of foil. Lay the parchment inside the foil and then wrap the shooter tightly. Put the whole thing into a container, place a weight on top and leave in the fridge overnight.

Next day, unwrap your shooter, take a serrated knife and cut yourself a wedge.

Alan Turing's Crumpets

You will need crumpet rings to achieve good-shaped crumpets. Feel free to use any metal circular or square moulds, depending on your preference.

Makes 8–10 crumpets

1 tablespoon caster (superfine) sugar
250 ml (8½ fl oz/1 cup) whole milk
250 ml (8 1/2 fl oz/1 cup) lukewarm water
2 tablespoons dried active yeast
125 g (4 oz) plain (all-purpose) flour
125 g (4 oz) strong white flour

2 teaspoons salt
1½ teaspoons bicarbonate of soda
   (baking soda)
1 tablespoon sunflower oil
Butter and Marmite, jam or cheese,
   to serve

Put the sugar, milk and 150 ml (5 fl oz) of the lukewarm water into a large mixing bowl and whisk to combine. Scatter in the yeast and mix well, then leave to one side in a warm place for 15 minutes or until you have a nice frothy mixture.

Gradually add the two flours to the frothy liquid, bit by bit, whisking all the time to avoid lumps. Keep whisking until you have a nice smooth batter, then cover with a clean tea towel and leave to prove for 45 minutes. When it is ready, a few bubbles should start to form on the top; if not, give the batter a bit more time, checking again after another 15 minutes.

In a separate bowl, mix the salt and bicarbonate of soda into the remaining 100 ml (3½ fl oz) of lukewarm water until dissolved, then stir this into the batter – it should start to rise straight away. Cover again and leave for another 20 minutes to get nice and lively.

When you're ready to cook the crumpets, place a heavy-based frying pan over a medium heat and turn on your grill (broiler) to high. Grease the moulds with the oil and place in the hot frying pan and allow to get hot.

Fill your pastry rings about two thirds full with batter. This should be about 4 tablespoons. Cook for 12 minutes without moving or turning. If you're worried it is burning turn the heat down, but don't forget, crumpets are meant to be dark on the bottom. The crumpets are ready to come out when the surface is full of bubbles and just set on top. Pick the crumpet and ring up with a spatula and put on a wire rack. When handleable, see if the ring just comes off; if it doesn't, cut around the perimeter of the crumpets with a sharp knife and re oil the ring for cooking more crumpets. Once you have cooked all the crumpets, place them on a baking tray and grill (broil) for a minute to colour the tops.

These are rather special hot. If you want to make like Alan Turing, slather them with cold butter and marmite. If you're jazzy, try 'nduja and honey – they're your crumpets, do whatever you like.

Breakfast Martini

Do yourself a favour and buy the best you can. Get that good, good marmalade and a decent gin. Also, keep your gin and triple sec in the freezer, and freeze a couple of martini glasses too. That frosted glass is a rare treat, and essential for a perfect martini – at breakfast, or any other time.

Makes 2 martinis

Ice
2 tablespoons fine-cut marmalade
100 ml (3½ fl oz) gin

2 tablespoons triple sec or Cointreau
2 tablespoons lemon juice
1 slice of bread, toasted

Put a few lumps of ice in a martini glass and fill it with water to chill.

Put the marmalade in a cocktail shaker with the gin and triple sec and stir and stir until the marmalade has dissolved.

Fill the shaker with ice, add the lemon juice and stir and stir and stir making sure the spoon goes right to the bottom of the shaker. Don't shake it like that philistine Bond, it will only water it down.

Stir 50 times - count them. The shaker will have become so frosty and cold you will hardly be able to touch it.

Sling the iced water from the glass and pour the sparkly liquid through a sieve into it.

On the side of your martini, have a slither of cold, heavily buttered toast with marmalade on it. Why should the toast be cold? Because as my mum says, 'Butter should be ON toast, not IN toast'.

HACKS

Eight things that really are a picnic,
but no one ever noticed

1. A meal at your desk

2. A meal on a train

3. A meal in a motorway service station

4. Something to eat at the airport

5. A midnight feast

6. Something to eat and/or drink on a nice long walk

7. Fish and chips on the beach

8. A packet of crisps in a pub garden

icnic

'If there's a sausage on the menu, Max will order it.' – Ned Halley, Max's dad

This picnic is dedicated to two things, Milly Mouse, for being the best dog ever, and lest I forget, my best friend in the whole world … the sausage. When it comes to the sausage my love is indiscriminate: I like the hangover-eviscerating, dubiously deep-fried Greasy Spoon ones cooked by Mustafa (page 102) every bit as much as the posh ones with fennel seeds you might buy in an Italian deli.

Milly Mouse loves sausages too, perhaps even more than I do. She is loyal in her desire to attack anyone she deems a threat to me, but alas, more loyal to the sausage. She will happily have a go at me if I have procured myself one and not shared the spoils.

Milly is not my dog. She belongs to my ex-girlfriend and dear friend Holly Chaves. I keep a photo of Milly in her Amelia Earhart costume on my phone and on the wall of my sandwich shop. Whenever I feel a bit down, I look at it and my spirit soars. You can see from her calm, steely-eyed confidence, she KNOWS she looks the bomb in that flying hat. If you're ever feeling a bit tender, reach for this book, turn to page three, and look at Milly in her flying gear and the darkness will begin to lift.

For Milly, this picnic is about bringing together her best friends for a catch up, having a bit of a giggle and celebrating the sausage and its infinite diversity.

She's pleased to see her friend Shergar, particularly after what happened. Shergar was one of the world's most valuable pieces of bloodstock and an ex-super-champion racehorse. In 1983 he was kidnapped for a £2 million ransom, which wasn't paid, and Shergar was never seen again.

Bebop and Rocksteady, infamous nemeses of the *Teenage Mutant Ninja Turtles*, are two of Milly's favourite baddies of all time. They're a right pair of plonkers to be honest, but they amuse her with their massive ghetto blaster (boom box)and tiny brains. Milly is extremely forgiving, she loves them wholeheartedly and we all have old friends we love but none of our new mates understand why we hang out with.

Milly's final guests at today's sausage-fest are Ratty and Mole from *The Wind in the Willows*, the best book about animals ever. If you don't know who Ratty and Mole are, put this book down, buy a copy of *The Wind in the Willows*, read it and I will meet you back here.

Oh gosh, yes, this picnic is about another thing too: leftovers! Not just because Milly and I both love leftovers, but because picnics love leftovers. Together, Ben and I would like to encourage just generally, the idea of making a delicious dinner for tonight, with a picnic in mind for tomorrow! All too often, in picnic situations, we're sold food that is neither appealing nor value for money. But armed with leftovers, we can rediscover these opportunities for deliciousness and reclaim the picnic!

MENU

Cotechino

Glamorgan Sausages

Braised Lentils

Mostarda
('Mustard Fruit')

Fantasy Host
Milly, in her Amelia Earhart outfit

Fantasy Guests
Ratty and Mole from *The Wind in the Willows*, Shergar, Bucephalus, Bebop and Rocksteady

Location
The gang are very close to where Ratty and Mole live, just the right side of the Wild Wood.

Dress Code
Come as your hero. Milly has.

Unpacking the Hamper

Milly knows nothing draws a crowd like a sausage and she has excelled herself today and brought the sausage to end all sausages: ladies, gentlemen and everyone, I give you ... the *cotechino*. A special treat indeed, the cotechino is a delectable, gelatinous sausage made from minced up skin and fat stuffed inside a pig's trotter. For real. It is traditionally eaten in Italy on New Year's Eve, served with lentils, sometimes polenta, and a big heap of those most jewel-like of foods, *mostarda* (mustard-preserved kiwi, chestnuts, apricots, quinces, peaches, pears, cherries, etc.).

Milly knows there'll be grumbles from Bebop and Rocksteady about the lentils, but they're seasoned up nicely, so they can do one. On the round-robin email, Milly asked all her guests to cook their favourite sausages for supper last night, so they could bring their stragglers along today.

Shergar is vegetarian, and his local shop was out of meat-free sausages, so rather wonderfully, he knocked up some Glamorgan sausages. Bebop has a few Polish kielbasa and Rocksteady a couple of North African merguez. Ratty and Mole had Mr-Toad-in-the-hole for tea, and cooked off a load of extra Cumberlands. Ratty put them in a Tupperware hot and popped them in the refrigerator because him and Mole have a mutual love of the gelatinous goo that forms when a sausage cools in Tupperware (Ratty mixes it into mayonnaise). Like my dad, Ratty thinks that marmalade is amazing with cold sausage, so he has brought along a jar for everyone to try with their bangers.

This picnic might be mostly sausages and lentils, but all the pulses – whether tinned, in cartons, or the posh ones in jars – are delicious. You can make them into a stew by frying off some onions and garlic (and anything else that might be lying about), throwing in a chicken stock cube dissolved in some boiling water and baking them in an oven until the liquid is nice and thick – it's that easy. When they're done, dress them liberally with olive oil and lemon juice and season generously with salt, then put them in the fridge overnight. The next day, stir through some fresh herbs and pack them up with your choice of leftover roast meat or aubergine (eggplant), a tin of tuna, a few boiled eggs or indeed a couple of sausages to go on the side. You'll be in picnic seventh heaven!

Invest in some Tupperware, or keep the plastic tubs from your Indian/Chinese takeaway (just remember to wrap them in cling film (plastic wrap) after refilling with your goodies to avoid seepage) and you can have a wonderful meal at your desk instead of buying a supermarket sandwich that is so bad they have to give you a free bottle of Coke and a packet of crisps to make up for it.

Braised Lentils

Good lentils are hard to beat: hot or cold; plain or with tasty bits and pieces stirred through them; served with a tablespoon of mustard or a lick of mayonnaise. Indulge yourself.

It is worth noting that these lentils will improve even further if left to cool and rest in the fridge overnight, before being reheated the following day.

Serves 8–10

250 g (9 oz) Castelluccio or Puy lentils (don't mess about with anything else)
1.5 litres (51 fl oz/6 cups) water
4 tablespoons extra virgin olive oil, plus extra to taste
1 onion, peeled and quartered
1 celery stalk, cut into thirds

2 bay leaves
4–5 sprigs of sage
1 teaspoon salt
1 tablespoon red wine vinegar
Cotechino and Mostarda (page 126), to serve

Soak the lentils in cold water for at least 30 minutes, then drain. Put them into a large saucepan with the water and add all the other ingredients except the salt and vinegar. Bring to the boil, then turn the heat down to a low simmer – blip, blip, blip – and cook like this for 45 minutes–1 hour. When the lentils are yielding but not soft, remove from the heat and stir in the salt and vinegar. Pop a lid on the pan and leave for 20–30 minutes.

Taste the lentils and their broth, then adjust the seasoning with salt and vinegar as needed, adding a little more olive oil, too, if you think they could be silkier. Once you are satisfied, pick out the bay leaves and any large pieces of the sage you can find. Serve warm, with a cotechino, some mustard fruits and polenta if the fancy takes you. To cook the cotechino just follow the instructions that come with it, which is normally just boiling it in the packet it comes in.

Glamorgan sausages

These fellas are the original and the best. Leeky, cheesy and crispy, they do a different job to a meaty banger, but deserve every bit as much respect, whether at a picnic or on the dinner table.

Makes 8 sausages

75 g (2½ oz) butter
150 g (5 oz) leeks, thinly sliced (about 1 large or 2 small leeks)
200 g (7 oz/2½ cups) fresh breadcrumbs
2 sprigs of thyme, leaves picked and chopped
225 g (8 oz) Caerphilly cheese (or any other strong and slightly sour cheese), grated or crumbled

2 free-range eggs, separated
2 teaspoons English mustard
3 tablespoons milk
Plain (all-purpose) flour, for dusting
Salt and freshly ground black pepper
Braised Lentils (page 123) and Mostarda (page 126), to serve

Place a large frying pan over a high heat and melt half the butter. When frothing, add the leeks and season with plenty of salt and pepper. Cook for 6–8 minutes, stirring regularly, until well softened.

Now throw half the breadcrumbs and all of the thyme into the pan. Stir well, then add the cheese and stir again. Stir in the egg yolks and mustard, followed by the milk. When everything is thoroughly combined, remove from the heat and set aside for about 5 minutes, until cool enough to handle.

With wet hands, shape the mixture into eight sausages, then chill for half an hour.

Meanwhile, preheat the oven to 180°C (350°F/gas 4) and prepare your breading station thus: whisk the egg whites with a fork until frothy, then take three shallow bowls or plates and put the whisked egg white in one, the flour in another and the remaining breadcrumbs in the last.

When you're ready, roll each sausage first in the flour, then the egg white and finally the breadcrumbs. If you're a crispy-crust craver, do a second round in the egg and crumbs.

Melt the remaining butter in an ovenproof frying pan over a medium heat. When hot, add the sausages and cook until lightly golden on each side, about 5 minutes. Transfer the pan of sausages to the oven and cook for about 20 minutes, or until they're golden brown.

Serve with the lentils (page 123) and mostarda (page 126).

Mostarda ('mustard fruit')

This mostarda recipe is not utterly authentic. To make mostarda authentically (as they do in Cremona in Italy) you have to use super concentrated mustard essence, which is genuinely dangerous (see Mustard Gas) and best left to the professionals. If you want some traditional mostards, buy some when you pick up your enormous cotechino sausage! As is becoming the norm in this book, you'll have to plan for this one. The fruit needs to be soaked in sugar for at least 24 hours, so think ahead and make this in a quiet moment. It will keep for decades, so don't fret that it takes some groundwork.

Makes enough to fill 3–4 x 500 ml (17 fl oz) jars

1 kg (2 lb 4 oz) assorted fruit (kiwi, fig, pear, apple and cherries would be traditional and work well – mix it up though, experiment!)

500 g (1 lb 2 oz) caster (superfine) sugar
2 tablespoons white wine
Juice of 1 orange
4 tablespoons mustard powder

Chop your fruit into large chunks – in half or quarters is usually fine. Put it into a bowl, add the sugar and toss gently, then leave in a cool, dark place for at least 24 hours and up to 48 hours, giving the fruit an occasional stir if and when you remember.

After this time, the sugar should have dissolved into the fruit to make a syrup. Drain the fruit in a sieve set over a pan. Set the drained fruit aside. Add the wine to the syrup in the pan and bring to a boil, then reduce the heat to low and simmer until the syrup is thick, glossy and reduced by half. Now is the time to add the orange juice and mustard powder, followed by the fruit, stirring gently to cover and coat it all.

Transfer the fruit to a sterilised jar and pour over the syrup, then seal the jar and leave for at least a week or up to 18 months in a dark place at room temperature.

To serve, remove the fruit and roughly chop, mixing through a little of the syrup. Once the jar is opened, store it in the fridge and use within 2 weeks.

HACKS

Six essentials for your 'hanging on the back of a door in a tote bag until the next big picnic day' picnic kit

1   A good selection of Tupperware in different sizes: all with clip lids.

2   A few Thermos flasks: small ones for cocktails and sauces, gravy, etc; larger ones for more serious food moments, or a load of Snickers ice-creams.

3   Four Duralex glasses wrapped in newspaper.

4   Four cutlery sets (knives, forks and spoons) and one steak knife: a steak knife will cut bread, lemons and the like much more easily than a table knife.

5   Four nice good-quality plastic plates.

6   One roll of cling film (plastic) wrap.

Note: *Most of this is stuff I have accumulated from charity (thrift) shops over the years. When you embark on a more organised picnic like this, take your car's picnic kitbag (page 23) with you too, leaving behind any duplicates. Might as well start the day armed to the teeth!*

A 'Hidden Potential' Picnic

9

The ability to look at something, see its potential,
and exploit it, is a feather in the cap of the picnicker.

In this fantasy land, we have brought together a selection of figures from the annals of criminal history to demonstrate how, when it comes to picnicking, we must put a little more creativity into thinking on our feet. And in the case of Joaquín 'El Chapo' Guzmán, Sandra Ávila Beltrán, Griselda Blanco and Pablo Escobar, where we see a crime, they see an opportunity – that's why these guys became so rich and powerful. I'm not encouraging anyone to start dealing drugs, unless they've got a shoe-in at Glaxo or something, but I am saying that to picnic like a kingpin, we could all learn something from this group. An ability to look at something, see its potential, and exploit it, is a feather in the cap of the picnicker.

It goes without saying that these people are absolutely terrifying but, damn, do they know how to do a bit of PR. El Chapo is often viewed (seemingly with little evidence) as a Robin Hood sort of character for his enrichment of local communities around his home, while Pablo Escobar does genuinely appear to have done a great deal for the poor in Colombia, particularly in Medellín. Figuring his great strength was the support of the people, he built schools, churches, hospitals, sports grounds and social housing before entering politics. I feel a little more potted history is needed before we dive in. Griselda Blanco was the 'Godmother of Cocaine', with an empire spanning most of the US. She was a certified badass, and not always in a good way – she was credited with slaying a large number of her enemies, and some innocent bystanders too.

Sandra Avila Beltran counts as cartel aristocracy. Born into the family of a senior cartel member, she married into a Mexican and then a Colombian drug cartel. It is no wonder she was widely thought to be the direct link between El Chapo's Sinaloa cartel and the Colombian Norte Del Valle cartel.

OK, now we're all up to speed, be prepared – in this trip around my head, we will go on to see El Chapo and the gang turn what would appear (and in fact, is) a few flasks of cold soup and a massive sausage, into a really fun and utterly delicious picnic.

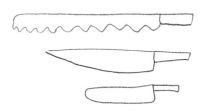

The Three Gazpachos

Mortadella

Michelada

Fantasy Host
'El Chapo'

Fantasy Guests
Sandra Ávila Beltrán, Griselda Blanco, Pablo Escobar

Location
Sometimes, being outside can calm a group, minimise tensions and avert any scuffles.

Dress Code
Everyone's had a long drive, so comfortable shoes and box-fresh driving gloves are required. I'd like to think that all four are wearing polarised sunglasses, too.

Unpacking the Hamper

Sandra never embarks on a long journey without her Thermos collection. She's got three with her today, filled with different gazpachos, and she heads to the car to get them.

Never one to miss an opportunity, all her Thermoses have removable bottoms too, like the shaving foam can in *Jurassic Park*.

Wary of an onlooker raising the alarm, she quickly pours a round of ice-cold gazpacho for everyone. Pablo takes a sip, leaving traces of the nectar in his moustache, and declares the soup 'very good indeed'. Griselda loves it too, and getting into the swing of things, decides to get her showstopper out. She has brought a whole mortadella and even El Chapo is impressed. He launches into a speech about how fantastic charcuterie is at a picnic. It doesn't mind being out of the fridge for hours at a time, and in fact improves as it warms up and the fat melts a little.

One of the simplest of breakfasts – and a personal favourite of mine – is a packet of croissants and two packets of Parma ham. The sweet croissants filled up with salty ham makes me happy and is an extremely delicious and achievable breakfast to have on a train or in the back of a car.

Griselda whips out a machete and deftly peels and slices, unbelievably thin, a good third of the giant mortadella. Everyone pigs out and comments on how the gazpacho is such a great foil to the delicious fatty meat. Great picnicking is like any successful meal, no matter how simple it might seem, it is about picking things that get along. Whenever you have something fatty, something acidic is always an excellent bedfellow. That's why lemon juice squeezed on bread and butter is so good; why sherry and jamón íberico like each other so much; and why fried chicken and hot sauce are the bestest of friends.

El Chapo heads to the car, he's had an idea. Like Hunter and Mary, he keeps a kitbag in his car's glove compartment, and in it, he's got everything he needs to make his famous Micheladas – barring the beer and Clamato, which are in the boot. He wishes He wishes they had some ice because the drink really needs it, but they don't.

If one can't be arsed with the rigamarole of making gazpacho like Sandra's (pages 137–139), finding a good-quality tomato juice adding seasoning directly into it through the spout is a very sage idea. Similarly, adding vodka and taking it from gazpacho to Bloody Mary will never be frowned upon – not by us, and not by this gang, either.

Also, DO make Micheladas! Have you had one before? The Michelada, is Mexico's version of the Bloody Mary, and in my opinion, a far superior drink. They are insanely refreshing on a hot day and fundamentally not that boozy so can put them away without doing anything too embarrassing. We sell so many at the Sandwich Shop, especially on Sundays, London's big Bloody Mary day.

Use a light refreshing lager to make your Michelada, and revel in the Clamato juice's unexpected, saline deliciousness. It sounds creepy (clam and tomato juice) but lest we forget, you put Lea & Perrins in your Bloody Mary (or on your crisps if you're Hunter S. Thompson) and that is essentially anchovy juice!

If you do insist on a Bloody Mary, try using gazpacho (or Clamato Juice) instead of tomato juice. It is less gloopy, much fresher and fundamentally, much more delicious.

HACKS

Seven good excuses to visit a fast-food restaurant when you are a semi-professional picnicker

1. They have a loo (toilet).

2. They have condiments on actual TAP.

3. Stealable salt and pepper sachets.

4. Little reusable cutlery items.

5. Napkins and wet wipes.

6. You can ask for cups of ice (SO USEFUL), as long as you've bought something.

7. You can just call the whole thing off and get a burger instead.

These are taken directly from Sandra Ávila Beltrán's Filofax, which is where she keeps all her handwritten recipes. She is said to prefer the classic at lunchtime, the green on a hot evening, and the white just after concluding business. All make enough for four people.

Green Gazpacho

Let's start with the green version.

100 g (3½ oz) slightly stale crusty white bread
1 kg (2 lb 4 oz) ripe yellow cherry tomatoes, diced
2 green (bell) peppers, deseeded and diced
1 medium cucumber, peeled and diced
1 stick of celery, diced

3 garlic cloves, crushed
1 large handful of coriander, leaves picked and torn
About 150 ml (5 fl oz) extra virgin olive oil
About 2 tablespoons sherry vinegar
Salt and caster (superfine) sugar, to taste

Cover the bread with cold water and leave to soak for 20 minutes.

Squeeze out the bread and put it straight into a food processor or blender, along with all the remaining ingredients except the vinegar, salt and sugar. Blend until fairly smooth.

Place a sieve over a large bowl and pass the gazpacho through the sieve, using the back of a spoon to work it through. Now add the vinegar and a good pinch of salt and give it a taste: depending on the sweetness of your tomatoes and peppers, you might want more vinegar or more oil; you may even want a small pinch of sugar to it.

When you are happy, cover it and let it chill in the fridge for at least an hour. You want this guy cold and refreshing.

Classic Gazpacho

Gazpacho is simplicity itself, but in order to be simple and good, you need to make sure each of your ingredients taste exceptional in themselves. Do not make this with out-of-season supermarket veg, or it will underwhelm and frustrate. Wait for a hot day in summer, and use tomatoes that smell of tomato and peppers that are firm and smell sweet. You'll want an olive oil with a delicious flavour, too. Other than that, go for your life.

You can serve this just as it is: perhaps with a few pieces of chopped pepper or cucumber if you're after a bit of texture and bite, perhaps with a few cubes of good Spanish ham for a salty kick. Sandra always eats this gazpacho with a hunk of burnt toast, liberally rubbed with garlic.

100 g (3½ oz) slightly stale crusty white bread
1 kg (2 lb 4 oz) very ripe tomatoes, diced
2 red (bell) peppers, deseeded and diced
1 medium cucumber, peeled and diced

3 garlic cloves, crushed
About 150 ml (5 fl oz) extra virgin olive oil
About 2 tablespoons sherry vinegar
Salt, to taste

Cover the bread with cold water and leave to soak for 20 minutes.

Squeeze out the bread and put it straight into a food processor or blender, along with all the remaining ingredients except the vinegar and salt. Blend until fairly smooth.

Place a sieve over a large bowl and pass the gazpacho through the sieve, using the back of a spoon to work it through. Now add the vinegar and a good pinch of salt and give it a taste: depending on the sharpness of your tomatoes, you might want more vinegar or more oil.

When you are happy with the lip-smacking greatness of your soup, cover it and let it chill in the fridge for at least an hour.

White Gazpacho

This is close to tipping over into *ajo blanco* territory, but I won't tell Sandra if you don't.

100 g (3½ oz) blanched almonds
100 g (3½ oz) slightly stale crusty white bread
500 g (1 lb 2 oz) green grapes, diced
2 medium cucumbers, peeled and diced
1 stick of celery, diced

3 garlic cloves, crushed
About 150 ml (5 fl oz) extra virgin olive oil
About 2 tablespoons sherry vinegar
Salt, to taste

Preheat your oven to 200°C (400°F/gas 6). Spread out the almonds on a baking tray (pan) and roast for 8 minutes, then allow to cool slightly and transfer to a small bowl. Add just enough cold water to cover the almonds and leave to soak for 20 minutes.

Cover the bread with cold water and leave to soak for 20 minutes.

Squeeze out the bread and put it straight into a food processor or blender, along with the almonds and their soaking water. Add all the remaining ingredients except the vinegar and salt and blend until fairly smooth.

Place a sieve over a large bowl and pass the gazpacho through the sieve, using the back of a spoon to work it through. Now add the vinegar and a good pinch of salt and give it a taste: depending on the sweetness of your grapes, you might want more vinegar or more oil.

When you are happy, cover it and let it chill in the fridge for at least an hour.

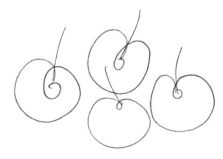

Michelada

The Michelada – the Mexican Bloody Mary. What a beverage! My dear Mexican friend Magali Bellego got me into these many years ago and I have never looked back. When she makes you one it has so much Tabasco, Lea & Perrins and Maggi in it, it is brown not red, but you don't have to make it like that! I would recommend making this in a jug (everything bar the beer), whether you are on your own or in company, as one Michelada is never enough.

Makes 4

2 tablespoons Tajín seasoning
   (or salt, lemon zest and chilli flakes,
   ground together)
4 limes, cut in half
500 ml (17 fl oz/2 cups) Mott's Clamato,
   if you can find it (or tomato juice
   or gazpacho)
1 tablespoon Tabasco sauce

2 tablespoon Worcestershire sauce
1 tablespoon Maggi sauce
4 x 330 ml (4 fl oz) bottles or cans of
   lager (Pacifico or Modello would be
   perfect but use whatever you like –
   it is a different, but lovely, drink when
   made with dark lagers too!)

Start with the glasses which ideally you will have wet under the tap and put in the freezer for 15 minutes (pint glasses would be perfect).

Personally, I don't like things on the rim of glasses, it makes me feel like Jim Carrey in Ace Ventura when he's eating the sunflower seeds in Courtney Cox's office, but many people loves it so do what you will.

Sprinkle the Tajin (or homemade equivalent) seasoning on a saucer or small plate. Run round the rim of your glass with a lime wedge, then dip it into the into the seasoning, making sure you get good coverage all the way round like in the photo.

Take a large jug and add the Clamato, Tabasco, Maggi, Worcestershire sauce and any leftover seasoning from the saucer. Squeeze in the juice from all four of the limes. Give everything a good stir. Fill your glass(es) with ice, and a straw and fill about fifty per cent with the Clamato mix.

Crack a beer and tip it in. Stir it. Sip it. Add a little more spice or anything if it tickles your fancy. There is no right answer on the seasoning front. It's personal preference. You should have lip puckering from the lime, a slight wince from the chilli and a deep sigh of refreshment from the beer. As you drink, keep adding more beer which means, due to dilution etc, the drink you end up with is not the same as the drink you started with, making Micheladas all the better.

'If you're afraid of butter, use cream.' Julia Child

Even if all of her that survived were her comments about food, eating and butter, Julia Child (1912–2004) would still be one of the greats. Along with her friend Simeone Beck, she was responsible for introducing French food to America. Firstly, through their magnum opus, *Mastering the Art of French Cookery*, and secondly, through a multitude of successful TV shows.

A huge fan of breaking bread and sharing the pleasures of the table, Julia has invited some of her favourite people to lunch in her mate Michelle Obama's garden.

Julia may not appear to have (butter-related) feelings about nutrition, but the nation's children weren't in such a physical pickle in the sixties as they are now. Julia loves what Michelle's done to the White House Garden and admires her feelings about growing and eating delicious fruit and vegetables. 'You don't have to cook fancy or complicated masterpieces,' Julia once said, 'just good food, from fresh ingredients.'

One of Julia's longstanding heroes, the Widow Clicquot, inherited a failing business at 27 on the untimely death of her husband, and turned it into the Champagne powerhouse that Veuve ('widow') Clicquot is today.

She did it by employing well, being one of the ballsiest sales people ever to have lived and being an entrepreneurial genius. She sold Champagne on the front line to both the French and Russian officers during the Napoleonic Wars, revolutionised the Champagne production process and became one of the richest woman in Europe along the way.

Next up it's Dolly Parton. Julia doesn't approve of her tattoos no matter how secret, but finds her verve, vigour and faultless songwriting talent utterly inspirational. And they have similar feelings about pork chops – Dolly is renowned for liking the fat and gristle on her chops. Disappointingly for Julia, Dolly prefers Taco Bell to most highfalutin dining establishments, but that just makes Julia all the more determined to get some decent food down her today.

Lastly is someone Julia is extremely excited about: Catherine the Great. Julia is a little starstruck by the woman who pulled off a *coup d'état* in Russia, under extremely hostile conditions, while devoting much of her time and attention to reading Voltaire, studying art history, drinking Champagne, selecting and being satisfied by her lovers, and (allegedly) designing some of the most erotic furniture imaginable.

MENU

Pesce Crudo ('Raw Fish')

Tortellini in Brodo

Zabaglione with Macerated Fruit

Fantasy Host
Julia Child

Fantasy Guests
**Madame Clicquot,
Michelle Obama, Dolly Parton,
Catherine the Great**

Location
**In fantasy land, we are in Michelle Obama's thriving
White House garden, which she completely revamped
and expanded. I suggest you find somewhere
similarly inspiring.**

Dress Code
**Wear anything you like – full state regalia like Catherine
the Great, perhaps.**

Unpacking the Hamper

As Julia's in charge, none of today's food is particularly pretty but it is outrageously delicious. Suspicious of beautiful food, she said, '[If it's] beautifully arranged on the plate, you know someone's fingers have been all over it.'

She wants everything to be top dollar, but doesn't want to be chained to the kitchen, so her and her beloved diplomat husband, Paul, have come up with three courses all doable in advance, delicious at room temperature and all the better for sitting around a bit. You might say, they are literally perfect picnic dishes.

The Widow Clicquot is in charge of the booze, of course, and guess what she's brought? That's right, enough Champagne to sink the Battleship Potemkin.

Catherine the Great's trumpeters herald the arrival of the food. Three baskets stacked on top of each other like wicker tiffin tins are put on the table. Before they get stuck in, Julia says they're going to have bread and butter. It's the good good bread Michelle's sorted – and the butter? 'Oh the butter!' Julia's having conniptions. Firstly, it is at room temperature, and secondly, it's that cultured yellow stuff with little salt crystals that crack between your teeth.

Julia pulls a plate piled high with iridescent slices of fish from the top basket. 'Pesce crudo,' she announces. 'Perfect with a little more of that bread, and a lot more of that butter.'

Fish dispatched, Julia dives into the next basket and surfaces with a large Thermos, a small ladle, and five bowls. She removes the lid from the flask and starts scooping inside with the ladle. She gives everyone three or four perfect parcels of meat filled pasta. 'Tortellini,' Julia announces salivating, 'in brodo.'

Having divided the pasta between the bowls, she pours just enough of the broth in so the pasta floats about a bit. Catherine reaches for the nearest bowl and receives a sharp slap on her wrist. 'Not just yet,' Julia snaps. 'A little grating of nutmeg and Parmesan first.'

Catherine thinks to herself that she wouldn't describe that as a LITTLE grating of anything.

Finally, it is time for pudding. Julia pulls another Thermos from the bottom basket. This one is filled with gorgeous Marsala-spiked zabaglione, and a Tupperware of luscious marinated fruit. Everyone goes in and the Widow tops everyone up with a magnum of Veuve's Demi-Sec to go with their pudding.

The Secret Service are all milling around a bit as they get the impression things are getting a little loose. Six magnums of Champagne have been sunk so far. Catherine's out cold and the Widow is drawing a moustache on her face.

Pack your own

This picnic's gone full high-brow hasn't it? There's even a recipe for making pasta!

Fret not, though, if that is your idea of BURNING IN THE FIERY PITS OF HELL, I have a way round all of it. All you need is a Thermos or two, and to have been shopping.

Buy a pack of tortellini from the store, fill a nice big Thermos half-full of boiling water, drop in a Parmesan rind (if you've got one), a big pinch of salt, and pour in a tin of store-bought beef consommé.

Sling the tortellini in and put the lid on. By the time you arrive at your picnic destination, you will have perfectly cooked tortellini and perfectly warm broth. Julia's nutmeg is a lovely touch if you can be arsed, and you could always take some grated Parmesan with you too. A little dried oregano, or marjoram, is also lovely.

If you can't face making Zabaglione, buy a tub of fresh custard from the fridge at the supermarket and tip some Marsala in it. It won't have the magic foamy-ness of the real thing, but you can warm it up, Thermos it and tip it on your fruit in the park nonetheless.

Tortellini in brodo

For those of you who, like Julia Child, take pride in doing things properly, here is a perfect tortellini in brodo recipe: the sort that you'd have to French-kiss a nonna for in Bologna.

There is no other way of saying this, but this recipe is a massive faff. There is a reason that this is a celebration dish in Emiglia-Romana, you need the whole family around to help roll the tortellini.

Serves 4 greedy diners

Freshly grated Parmesan and nutmeg, to serve

For the broth
500 g (1 lb 2 oz) chicken wings
1 onion, roughly chopped
1 carrot, peeled and chopped into chunks
2 celery stalks, chopped into chunks
1 Parmesan rind (you can cut this from the piece of Parmesan you will be grating later)
2.5 litres (80 fl oz/10 cups) water
Salt

For the pasta dough
200 g (7 oz) '00' flour, sifted, plus extra for dusting
2 medium free-range eggs

For the filling
300 g (10½ oz) minced (ground) pork – preferably shoulder, minced by your butcher
75 g (2½ oz) lardo, finely chopped
150 g (5 oz) prosciutto, finely diced
75 g (2½ oz) Parmesan, finely grated
2 eggs, lightly beaten
¼ nutmeg, freshly grated
2 teaspoons salt
2 teaspoons freshly ground black pepper

You're in for a marathon here, so let's start with an easy win by making the broth. In a massive saucepan, combine all the ingredients with the water and bring to the boil over a medium heat. Reduce the heat to low, skim off any scum that rises to the surface and simmer for 2 hours, continuing to skim the broth as and when needed. Allow the broth to cool slightly before straining it through a sieve and leaving it to one side.

While the stock is simmering, you'd better make the pasta dough – do not be overwhelmed, making pasta is simpler than you think. Dump your flour in a pile on a clean worktop and make a well in the middle. Crack the eggs into the well and whisk with a fork, gradually bringing the flour into the well as you go. Soon enough, you'll be able to get your hands in there to form a dough. Keep kneading until you have a smooth ball, then flatten it slightly, wrap in cling film (plastic wrap) and place in the fridge to relax while you make the filling.

We are motoring now. Next up is the filling: simply combine all the ingredients in a bowl and use your hands to bring it together. To check the seasoning, break off a little piece of the filling and quickly cook it in a frying pan, then give it a taste and add more salt, pepper and nutmeg to the rest of the filling as you see fit.

Now for the big one. Divide your pasta dough into three pieces and roll each one into a ball. If you have a pasta machine, now is its time to shine. Roll out the pasta, working your way down through the sizes, until you have an almost-translucent sheet. Taking one sheet at a time (and keeping the rest covered with a clean tea towel to prevent the pasta drying out), spread it out over a well-floured work surface and cut into 6 cm (2½ in) squares. Working quickly now, place a teaspoonful of the filling onto each square. You might want to watch a YouTube video here, but essentially you want to Fold the pasta diagonally in half over the filling to form a triangle, then fold the two pointier ends together and press – dab on a little water with your finger if needed to seal. You should have something that looks like the pope's hat or a folded napkin at a tacky dinner party. Keep going with the remaining pasta sheets and filling.

All that is left to do now is reheat the broth to a gentle simmer, drop in the tortellini and cook them for about 3 minutes – they are ready when they float to the surface.

Divide the tortellini between the bowls and top up with the broth. Serve with a liberal grating of Parmesan, and a little extra nutmeg if you think it needs it.

Pesce Crudo ('Raw Fish')

Ultimately, this one is all about keeping it simple and enjoying the deliciousness of fresh fish – a surefire way to bring happiness to you and your guests. For an extra flourish, you could scatter some very finely sliced dill, mint or coriander, a crunch of black pepper or a little chilli (freshly chopped or dried flakes).

Makes enough for 6

500 g (1 lb 2 oz) super-fresh sea bass fillet or other firm white fish, any skin removed (a friendly fishmonger can do this for you)

Finely grated zest of 1 large lemon
Maldon sea salt, to taste
Lemon juice and extra virgin olive oil, to serve

Using a very sharp knife, finely slice the fish at a 45-degree angle, skin-side down, to give you thin, almost translucent strips. You'll find this easiest if the fish is very cold and taken straight from the fridge.

Place your sliced fish on a platter and season with the lemon zest and salt, making sure each piece of fish gets a few flakes.

That is it, basically, and it makes a refined way to start any picnic. Just before eating, we would recommend a squeeze of lemon juice and a drizzle of olive oil.

Zabaglione with Macerated Fruit

This is a luxurious way to end any meal, let alone a picnic. There are challenges to transporting it, but a Thermos flask, or any other double-walled vessel should keep it warm for up to 2 hours. You may want to give it a quick shake before serving, but that's hardly too much to ask, is it, to have zabaglione out and about? This is one of the nicest, most comforting things in the entire world. VIVA ZABAGLIONE!!!

Serves 4

4 egg yolks
3 tablespoons soft brown sugar
4 tablespoons Marsala or dessert wine
Pinch of salt

For the macerated fruit
300 g (10½ oz) stone fruit and/or
    berries, such as cherries, apricots,
    strawberries and raspberries
1 tablespoon caster (superfine) sugar

First prepare your fruit: cut cherries in half, apricots and strawberries into halves or quarters, depending on their size, and leave raspberries whole. Put all the fruit into a glass bowl, sprinkle over the sugar and gently toss together. Cover and leave to macerate while you make the zabaglione.

You're going to want to work fast from here, so have everything weighed out and to hand.

Bring a 5 cm (2 in) depth of water to the boil in a saucepan. Find a heatproof bowl that will sit on top of the pan without its base touching the water (this is essential, or your zabaglione will curdle).

Take the bowl off the pan and add the egg yolks and sugar. Now whisk them like a demon for about 3 minutes, or until the mixture has doubled in volume and is thick and creamy.

Now add the booze and salt to the bowl. Carefully place the bowl over the pan of simmering water and continue to whisk, scraping down the sides of the bowl as you do so. After another 1–2 minutes of whisking, the whisk should leave defined ribbons in the mixture.

If you are eating straight away, divide your macerated fruit between individual bowls and spoon over the zabaglione. If you are picnicking, pour the zabaglione into a Thermos and seal. Pop your macerated fruit into a Tupperware and off you go.

HACKS

Six things you never thought to put in a Thermos flask – it keeps hot things hot and cold things cold!

1 **Perfect scrambled eggs:** slightly undercook your eggs and put in your Thermos. On the train: plate out, cold toast, cutlery GO GO GO HA HA HA.

2 **G'n'T with ice and lemon,** perhaps a Gibson or a Cosmopolitan: heading into the wilderness, but know you'll be in need of an ice-cold sharpener later? The Thermos is your friend. Of course, the same goes for hot chocolate, coffee and tea.

3 **Carbonara or *cacio e pepe*:** pre-load your Thermos with grated Parmesan (or pecorino), an egg yolk or two, some fried bacon (or just salt) and loads of pepper, then add hot pasta straight from the pan and a touch of the cooking water. Lid on and shake.

4 **Your favourite stew or curry:** take leftovers with you in your trusty Thermos. Ditch the terrible sandwich in a train station and eat something really delicious instead.

5 **Instant ramen noodles:** boil the kettle and wang everything into the Thermos, including some shredded spring onions, leftover meat, etc. Lid on and lunch like an absolute BOSS.

6 **Porridge:** measure oats into your Thermos, add three times the volume of hot water or milk, plus salt or sugar to taste. Lid on. Head out. Shake occasionally, and an hour later you'll have perfect porridge.

Note: *For chilled or frozen things, put the empty Thermos in the freezer with the lid off for half an hour beforehand.*

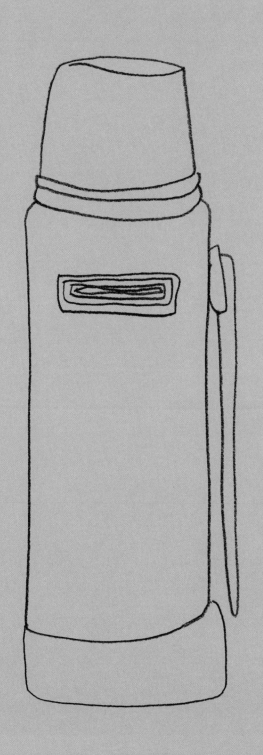

A 'Who Says a Loa
Can't be a Picnic?'

'One must be of one's time and paint what one sees.'
Édouard Manet

# of Boiled Eggs
icnic

This is an intimate picnic '*a deux*'. It is a picnic outdoors, in a green open space. It is a picnic where there doesn't need to be constant chatter; a picnic where something else altogether is taking place; a picnic where quiet contemplation, peaceful concentration, gentle conversation are fine, completely fine. These two men are wonderful artists, and they would recognise each other as such in a heartbeat. There is no competition between them, just mutual respect. They compete with one thing and one thing only, Mother Nature, and they know that she will always be the most accomplished artist of them all.

Born in 1955, in Birmingham, Alabama, Kerry James Marshall paints like a dream; his pictures are of such scale, structure, beauty and quality as to position him comfortably at the summit of the painters' pantheon.

For the sensibilities and traditional ideals of 1860s Paris, Édouard Manet's paintings, starting with *Le Déjeuner sur l'Herbe*, completed in 1863, were ideologically revolutionary. At the time, large paintings (of the scale both Manet and Marshall paint at) were considered to be the preserve of religious and historical figurative art, not for the portrayal of boozy picnics in the park. Nudes were allowed, even encouraged, but only if the figures depicted were goddesses or something of that ilk. An everyday woman? With normal clothes, casually discarded? IMAGINE! But, just like Marshall, what Manet wanted to do was to eat away at what the definition of acceptable subject matter was – and it worked.

Today, these two are picnicking outdoors: *en plein air*, if you will, as portrayed in their works. Their plan is to share a nice quiet lunch, and to look and learn from each other. They might talk occasionally – a compliment here, a technical question there – and maybe dab a boiled egg in some flavoured salt in between times.

Neither of them are big on blowing their own trumpets, so you won't hear them saying that *Le Déjeuner sur l'Herbe* changed the world of art forever, or that Marshall's 1997 masterpiece, *Past Times*, surpasses any previous exploration of white culture, or Western society's attitudes to race, visibility, absence and oppression.

What you will hear them both say is: 'Bloody hell/ *Zut alors*, I wish we'd brought some napkins – that's gone all over my shirt.'

MENU

Boiled Eggs with Flavoured Salts

Fish Soup

Fennel Salad

Absinthe

Perfect Pastis

Fantasy Host
Kerry James Marshall

Fantasy Guest
Édouard Manet

Location
The park, of course! A nice one with a lake, enough room for golf, croquet, water skiing and a bit of nudity.

Dress Code
Manet paints in a bonnet and pinafore; Kerry James Marshall in a nice shirt, cosy jumper and some jeans.

Unpacking the Hamper

Our Fantasy Host Kerry James Marshall has brought the very picnic basket he used as the model for the one in *Past Times*, and from it he whips out a little jar of tapenade, some garlic mayonnaise (YES!) and a load of croutons. Manet nods his approval at all these items. But when Kerry gets his Thermos out, Manet – quite understandably for someone born in 1832 – loses it!

'Kerry, what the hell is that?' he shouts.

'You don't know what a Thermos flask is, Édouard? It's a miracle of modern science!'

'What does it do?' Manet asks, edging closer.

'As I said, it's a miracle of modern science. It keeps hot things hot, and cold things cold.'

'NO?!' Manet is incredulous. 'What have you got in there?'

Marshall looks at Manet seriously and says: 'A cup of tea and a choc ice!' Hahahahahhahahahahh.

'Only joking, Édouard; it's *soupe de* bloody *poisson*, mate. I didn't make it though, are you joking? It's one of those big cloudy jars they have in posh fishmongers in England, and in all French supermarkets.'

Pouring a couple of bowls of soup, Marshall scatters croutons into the bowls and dabs them with tapenade and his famous garlic mayo.

Whatever you do, don't let cookbooks or chefs on TV tell you that you need to make your own mayonnaise. Life is too short, and there's NOTHING wrong with Hellmann's! The best garlic mayonnaise in the world is a couple of cloves of garlic, finely grated, mooshed with some salt and mixed into Hellmann's. End. Of.

Kerry's brought a small Tupperware of fennel salad with him too. It's an absolute blinder with the soup and goes extremely well with the absinthe and pastis Manet's got in his basket.

Soup finished, Manet says it's time for the main event and breaks out the big guns – his boiled eggs. He has a beautiful wooden box, filled with egg boxes, each filled with boiled eggs. Dalí would be proud. He also has a separate little box full to the rafters with paper wraps, concealing a multitude of delectable flavoured salts, all neatly labelled.

As the afternoon progresses, both artists take turns to grab an egg, deftly peel it, choose a wrap of salt, open it and dunk their egg in – what fun! Manet's only other concession to sustenance is that bottle of absinthe, which he's drinking by smashing a cheap white sugar cube into his glass, stirring until it's dissolved in the absinthe, and then adding a splash of water.

Kerry James Marshall has gone for pastis, as the absinthe is a bit much. Manet explains that even though Pastis is an incredibly simple drink, there is a perfect way to do it that should never be messed with.

Fish soup, boiled eggs, flavoured salts, pastis and absinthe – this is turning into a jolly.

Pack your own

Hard-boiled eggs can't be beaten for portability, and they couldn't be easier to cook. Just boil medium eggs in a large saucepan of boiling water for 7 minutes EXACTLY (7½ minutes for large eggs), then run them under cold water for a few minutes and pack into empty egg boxes.

HACKS

Six things to mix into salt

Flavoured salts are handy for pepping up a bag of crisps, shop-bought sandwiches, fried chicken, boiled eggs, etc. Make your choice of flavourings, then turn the page for info on how to doctor your salt…

1 Celery seeds – from wholefood shops, then coarsely ground

2 Smoked paprika

3 Curry powder

4 Sumac

5 Chilli flakes and finely grated lime zest

6 Garlic powder

Salts for Boiled Eggs

As per Manet's lifetime of experimentation, the key here is to try things. Below is a very simple formula to stick to, but with that as your only constraint, flavour-wise, you can go as far and wide as you desire, as you dare to dream. See where your taste buds take you. Mix a few things together, always sticking to the proportions below. Try half and half: garlic and chilli, paprika and finely grated lime zest, bonito flakes and yuzu. The internet, cookbooks, restaurant menus – they are all your friends here. Seek out flavours you've enjoyed, trawl through your memories of tastes and re-create them in salt.

Manet likes his salts on eggs, finding they make the perfect canvas for the flavours to sing. You might find that too, but don't limit yourself. Nice veg, boiled or roasted, is delicious dinked in a tasty salt, as are little chunks of boiled meat, the nub-end of a sausage, a prawn hot off the grill. Explore – that is the key.

1 part something else (fennel seeds, celery seeds, juniper berries, garlic powder, chilli powder, citrus zest, thyme, sumac, etc.)
2 parts sea salt

Find yourself a measure. Any measure will do: a teaspoon, tablespoon, thimble or trug. You'll also need a pestle and mortar or a spice grinder. Other than that, your imagination is the only thing you'll need. Start by measuring out your something else. Add one measure of this to your mortar or spice grinder and start to grind it to a rough powder, then add the salt and work it into the thing you've just ground. (Or, easiest of all, use a jam jar with a screw-top lid and shake like crazy.) When you have a pretty homogenous salt, you're all set.

Store the salt in an airtight jar or container, using it as and when the fancy takes you.

Fennel Salad

This is the freshest salad you'll ever eat. Any doubters when it comes to fennel need to leave those doubts at the door.

Makes enough for 2 people

1 fennel bulb, thinly sliced,
  any fronds reserved
Juice of 1 orange, ideally a blood orange

1 tablespoon extra virgin olive oil
Large pinch of salt

Slice your fennel as thinly as humanly possible. A sharp knife is fine, a mandoline is finer still. Be careful, obviously. Run a knife through any fronds from the fennel.

Place the sliced fennel in a bowl and hit it with the orange juice, oil and salt. Work the dressing into the fennel with your fingers. You then want to leave it alone for 5–10 minutes to let the citrus work its magic on the fennel.

Before you eat, stir through any fennel fronds and have a taste: does it need a little more orange juice, a crunch more salt? Other than that, eat away. Or pop it into a Tupperware and eat later. That is the joy with this salad – it's as good now as it will be tomorrow, or the day after that. (It will keep for up to 2 days in the fridge).

Perfect Pastis

We are old hands at pouring the perfect pastis, and as such are instinctive mixers, but if you would like a little guidance until you get better acquainted with this little zinger, follow the measurements below.

Makes 1 drink – multiply up as needed

20 ml (1½ tablespoons) pastis
100 ml (3½ fl oz/scant ½ cup) ice-cold water

Find a tall glass and pour in the pastis. Pour in the ice-cold water, enjoying the cloudy effect of the water on the liquor. (You do not want any actual ice here, as it will lock up the flavour of the pastis, leaving it tasting flatter than it should.)

Sip, sip, hooray. Drink, repeat. This tastes best when you're outside, throwing a heavy metal ball towards a little wooden ball.

An 'In The Mood Feast' Snacktrava

You can be serious about food, without taking food seriously.

When he was five, Wong Kar-wai's family moved from Shanghai to the Tsim Sha Tsui area of Hong Kong, home to the notorious Chungking Mansions and a focal point of the city's food culture. So it is perhaps unsurprising that his magnum opus, *In The Mood For Love*, grew out of a project he called 'Three Stories About Food' – this might give you an idea of how prominent a role food plays in the film.

A great deal of snacking goes on there too, and in our fantasy picnic, it is this that gives the great man himself the idea to throw a midnight feast of a birthday party. To help out, he has invited a load of his favourite chefs and is opening up his home to them.

As a film maker, Wong Kar-wai seems to believe that we are all mostly too weak to give things a go when we really desire them – to admit the strength of our feelings for the people we love or, conversely, to tell someone to piss off when they are ruining our lives. His (and my) stance is that if we were to grab more of the opportunities that present themselves to us, or even to notice them in the first place, we would have a far better, more satisfying life.

Hence him going hell-for-leather in my fantasy picnic plan – a cacophony of incredible chefs and food writers, to celebrate the duality of perfect picnic food: simplicity and seriousness.

MENU

Potato Samosas
Egg Salad Sandwiches
Pork Scratchings
Fine Red Wine

Fantasy Host
Wong Kar-wai

Fantasy Guests
**Harold McGee, Madhur Jaffrey,
Jeong Kwan, Anthony Bourdain,
Alan Davidson, Mason Hereford,
Keith Floyd**

Location
**Our gang are prepping in Wong Kar-wai's kitchen,
having fun with his snack drawer, larder and fridge, before
heading out to picnic on his balcony. balcony. Nat King Cole
(Wong's mother's favourite singer) is soundtracking the
evening, just as he unknowingly did *In The Mood For Love*.
After watching the film, Cole's beautiful voice, singing
in Spanish, will be burnt into your memory as strongly
as the images and message.**

Dress Code
**Pyjamas and sunglasses. Wong Kar-wai is never seen
without sunglasses on.**

Unpacking the Hamper

RING, RING!! 'Hello, this is Wong Kar-wai,' each call starts. 'It's my birthday and I'm throwing a midnight feast. I love your cooking and would like you to join me and make some snacks.'

After realising it isn't a prank, there is a sharp intake of breath from everyone and an immediate acceptance. The guestlist is soon filled, and it looks like this:

1   Harold McGee, the greatest mind to ever think about lunch
2   Madhur Jaffrey, a seminal writer and TV cook who tried to teach the British what real Indian food was.
3   Jeong Kwan, a Korean Buddhist nun and chef, capable of the most simple, delicate expressions of deliciousness on the planet.
4   Anthony Bourdain, an inspiration to us all.
5   Alan Davidson, writer of the best, most complete, amusing and brilliantly useful book ever written about food, *The Oxford Companion to Food.*
6   Mason Hereford, my American spirit animal: sharer of initials, owner of Turkey and the Wolf, and New Orleans-based sandwicher of great repute.
7   Keith Floyd: 90 per cent red wine, 10 per cent butter, and all the more enjoyable for it.

Having finished a marathon session of the director's back catalogue, everyone is a bit bleary-eyed, but exhilarated, and all too aware of the frailty of the human condition. As Wong has taught everyone, if you don't seize whatever it is you wish for when it makes an appearance in your life, when you return to it later, it will have shrivelled and died.

Sensing his fantasy feast is within his grasp, our host gathers the crowd in his kitchen and gives them free reign to create whatever they want. We can imagine Harold McGee contemplating for a while, unsure of what the best midnight snack might be: what combination of textures, sensations and flavours will sate and enliven, while also promoting a satisfying slumber in an hour or so? He rummages, he murmurs, he ponders. In the end, he admits he's not much of a late-night snacker and just has a glass of water and some well-chosen, perfectly ripe grapes and cherries. 'Sometimes, when everything seems to be about cooking,' he explains, 'it's best to do no cooking at all. Just eat stuff when it's ready.'

Madhur Jaffrey is a whirlwind of activity. She's frying tiny cubes of potato with onion and a blend of spices that are very reminiscent of Wong's beloved Chungking Mansions. Before you know it, she has a line of perfectly formed samosas ready to deep-fry. Watching in awe, Wong notes the same deftness and lightness of touch that Maggie Cheung has when she caresses walls, doorbells or Tony Leung's hand in *In the Mood for Love*.

Jeong Kwan travels with a few favourite things. She has a young miso paste, a little of her preferred soy sauce and some fermented long beans with her today – all true to her patient and carefully considered manner. Finding a couple of packs of udon noodles in Wong's cupboard, she boils them in the traditional way. In a bowl, the miso is mixed into the soy sauce and the drained noodles are added, then the long beans are chopped and tossed through to create the most mindful snack imaginable.

Anthony Bourdain and Alan Davidson are getting on like a house on fire. Alan reminds Anthony of Fergus Henderson somehow. Kindred spirits, they agree only three things are needed for a midnight snack, and Wong has them all: a bottle of export-strength Guinness, cold from the fridge, made-from-scratch pork scratchings and a two packets of cigarettes.

Mason Hereford, who normally makes sarnies more akin to meals than snacks, has got this one NAILED. He's making egg salad sandwiches, one of the simplest most delicious, pleasurable things to eat in the world. He sets a timer for the eggs he's boiling and has a rummage in Wong's bread bin. There's all sorts! Sourdough (NEVER), rye, brioche, crappy sliced white and the Japanese milk bread *shokupan*. 'Shokupan' he shouts, arms in the air. 'PERFECT!'

Shokupan is coincidentally extremely similar to Turkey and the Wolf's signature Pullman-type bread, both being made with milk.

He slices the springy white Japanese loaf, peels the eggs and forks them into some Duke's Mayo. A grind or two of salt and pepper, then tucks it all between the bread. When he cuts his perfect, soft and gentle egg sandwiches in half and holds up the cross-section for inspection, Tony Bourdain purrs with pleasure, as a true fan of the simple, delicious things in life.

While everyone else has been beavering away, Keith Floyd seems to have found the wine. Never one to dither, it appears that he's had a go at anything expensive-looking. At the end of the evening, when everyone is leaving, Wong enquires if Floyd has had enough to eat. Floyd assures his host that he's had a nibble of cheese and that'll do, explaining that he doesn't have much of an appetite late at night. Later that evening, when Wong is putting the remnants of the SNACKTRAVAGANZA away in the fridge, he discovers the lid of his cheese Tupperware ajar... Inside, every single cheese is unwrapped, with a large, red-wine-fringed bite taken out of the nose of each one... 'Floyd!!' Wong shouts from the balcony out into the darkness of the city.

I'm not sure what to say about this one, because it's all just snacks, isn't it?! As long as you don't eat so many you do yourself a mischief, snacks are one of the most fun, indulgent and lovely bits of – eating and you know what you like best.

Excellent samosas can be bought frozen from shops and supermarkets these days, and are a BADASS thing your freezer should never be without. And when you buy fruit, wait for it to be ripe before you eat it.

Eight easy-peasy cheese(y)cakes

This idea, from legend Coralie Sleap, is literally the perfect picnic pudding, as everything is ready-made and comes straight from a packet or jar. These things are as good on a blanket in a park as they are on a train, getting trashed with your mates in a car park, or sitting on the sofa with your mum watching the Olympics. The variations are almost infinite, but here are eight combos to get you started.

Top your chosen biscuit with dairy or marshmallow-y goodness, followed by the other ingredient/s. For a final flourish, try a sprinkling of crushed biscuits or nuts, malt powder or cocoa, perhaps a drizzle of that pomegranate molasses in your picnic kitbag (page 23). Now eat!

1 **Digestive, mascarpone, apricot jam**

2 **Ginger nut, ricotta, lemon curd**

3 **Hobnob, cream cheese, Biscoff spread**

4 **Dark chocolate Digestive, ricotta, cherry jam**

5 **Oreo, Marshmallow Fluff, glacé cherry**

6 **Jaffa cake, ricotta, marmalade**

7 **Garibaldi biscuit, mascarpone, dates, maple syrup**

8 **Malted milk, cream cheese, banana, salted caramel**

Potato Samosas

How good are samosas at a picnic? They're even better when you make your own.

Makes 20 samosas

1 x 270 g (9½ oz) pack of filo pastry
About 2 litres (8 cups) rapeseed (canola)
  oil, for deep-frying

For the filling
100 g (3½ oz) butter, 3 tablespoons
  more, melted, for samosa construction
1 large white onion, diced
750 g (1 lb 10 oz) waxy potatoes, peeled
  and diced
2 teaspoons garam masala
1 teaspoon ground cumin
1 teaspoon chilli powder
½ teaspoon ground turmeric
2 teaspoons salt
Juice of 1 lemon
Handful of mint leaves, torn

Start by heating the butter in a large frying pan. Add the onion and fry, stirring occasionally, for 10 minutes or until soft and golden. Add the potato and cook for a further 10 minutes, then add the garam masala, cumin, chilli powder, turmeric, salt and lemon juice. Stir to coat and cook for a couple more minutes, then take off the heat and allow to cool. Once cool, add the mint leaves and stir well.

To make the samosas, unroll a sheet of filo and place it on a large chopping board. Brush it lightly with melted butter and layer with another sheet of pastry. Cut the sheets into three horizontal strips.

You might want to watch a YouTube video of how to roll samosas, but essentially you make a conical shape at one end of the strip of filo, place 1 heaped tablespoon of the filling inside the cone, then fold the open side of the cone into the rest of the filo strip to cover and seal it. Keep folding over the rest of the pastry around the shape of the cone until you come to the end of the strip. Cut off any excess pastry and stick the strip down with a brush of melted butter. Pop the samosa on a tray and repeat.

All you need to do now is deep-fry your samosas. Pour the oil into a large, heavy-based saucepan and heat it to 180°C (350°F). (If you don't have a thermometer, test the temperature with a small piece of filo dropped into the oil: it should fizz and turn brown in about 5 seconds. Any quicker and your oil is too hot, any slower and it's not hot enough.)

Fry the samosas, three at a time, for about 3 minutes or until golden brown, lifting them out on to a baking tray (pan) lined with paper towels to drain. Eat hot, warm or cold for all I care, these are sensational regardless of temperature.

Egg Salad Sandwich

This is ridiculously simple and ridiculously satisfying. The simplicity is such that it could arguably be silly having a recipe for it, but getting it just right is such a joy. And what is the point of life, if you don't make the most of simple opportunities for deliciousness?

Makes 1 sandwich

3 hard-boiled, free-range eggs
1 teaspoon vingear (rice vinegar, if possible)
3 generous tablespoons Kewpie mayonnaise, or Duke's

2 slices soft white bread (ideally brioche or the Japanese milk bread called *shokupan*), crusts removed
Salt and white pepper

You can boil your eggs however you like, but we'd suggest a little update on your run-of-the-mill, water-in-pan-and-boil method. Add the vinegar to a saucepan of water and bring to the boil. Gently place the eggs in the water and boil, uncovered, for 6½ minutes. Immediately lift out the eggs and plunge into a bowl of cold water, leaving them there for a couple of minutes before peeling.

Smash with a fork or a potato masher for a few seconds, then taste and add more salt and pepper or a drop of vinegar if you believe it necessary. Spread the egg mayo thickly over one slice of bread, leaving a narrow border all around the edges – you want room for the egg to move when you bite into it without spilling out all over the floor.

Cut the third egg in half, top to bottom and place the halves next to each other in the centre of the sandwich. Put the lid. Cut the sandwich into thirds aiming for the centre of the yolks. Nice.

Pork Scratchings

First up, you'll need to have a conversation with your butcher, in order to get your hands on some pork rind (the skin of the pig, with a nice layer of fat attached underneath). Although this isn't an under-the-counter job, they likely won't have any on display – but they'll be delighted to sell you some, so just ask, or call ahead.

Makes enough to share with
a friend or two over a cold beer

100 g (3½ oz) pork rind
1 tablespoon salt

Preheat the oven to 170°C (340°F/gas 3).

Holding the pork rind skin-side down on a chopping board, run a sharp knife through the fat to create a chessboard of lines. Don't cut right through, just down to the skin. Sprinkle the salt onto the pork fat, forcing it into the slashes with your fingers.

Using sharp scissors, cut the pork rind into nice chunks about 2 cm (¾ in). Spread out the rinds on a baking tray skin side down, then pop in the oven.

As they roast, they'll release loads of fat, so spoon this out occasionally (you can keep it in the fridge and use it for frying eggs/cooking roast potatoes/pork chops etc).

Cook the scratchings for 45 minutes–1 hour, or until they are hard and crispy, then remove and put on a plate lined with paper towels.

Eat immediately, or store in an airtight container for up to 30 days.

nic

Unbeknown to most, Liberace released a brilliant book about himself cooking in 1970, called *Liberace Cooks!* – I might be the only person ever to call it 'the best book about sauces, gravy, soup and gazpacho since the Bible' but that's what it is. 'It's the sauces,' he writes, 'that divide the men from the boys, and separate the gourmets from the guzzlers.'

So, in celebration of the man who taught Elton John what dress sense was, who showed Jimi Hendrix how to do velvet, LADIES, GENTLEMEN and EVERYONE, I bring you a picnic in honour of the BIG GUN OF GLAMOUR, THE O.G. KING OF BLING, iiiiiittttttttt'ssssss LLLIIIIIIBBEERRAACCEE!!! Fireworks, glitter cannons, man on a wire, boom, boom, boom, bang, bang, bang, etc.

Our guests at this fantasy picnic need no introduction … but they're gonna get one anyway!

Sammy Davis Jr. was undoubtedly one of the greatest dancers, impressionists, entertainers and cigarette smokers of his generation. The appealingly middle-of-the-road Liberace may have been Vegas's biggest earner, but Sammy was the greater talent. Seriously good at all the things Liberace was silly at, he was a man who broke barriers like New Year's resolutions and danced like Dean Martin drank, LADIES, GENTLEMEN and EVERYONE, I GIVE YOU, LIVE FROM THE

PICNIC BLANKET OF DESTINY, Sammy, Davis, JJJUUUUUUNNNNIIIOOOORRRRRRR!!!!!!

'Miss West, are you trying to show contempt for this court?'

'No,' she said. 'I was doin' my best to hide it.'

Locked up for ten days on obscenity charges in 1927 for putting on a play called *Sex*, Mae West went in to prison a little notorious and came out of it famous. Only inside for eight days, she was released two days early for 'good behaviour' and treated the place like a holiday camp: she dined with the warden and his wife, and revelled in revealing that she'd worn silk knickers beneath her prison outfit. LADIES, GENTLEMEN and EVERYONE, I bring you a picnic with the ONE WOMAN SEXUAL REVOLUTION, the QUEEN OF BANTS AND PRISON SILK PANTS, the woman who SINGLE-HANDEDLY KEPT THE CENSOR'S OFFICE BUSY, iiiiiittttttt's MMMAAAAEEE WEEEEEST!!!!

Chicken Soup
Pickle-y Fries
Bourbon Milkshake

Fantasy Host
Liberace

Fantasy Guests
Sammy Davis Jr., Mae West

Location
The back of Liberace's Roller – *naturally, darling*

Dress Code
**Given Liberace's uncanny and hilarious resemblance to the
Count von Count Muppet from *Sesame Street* and Al Lewis'
as Grandpa in *The Munsters*, we're going full 'House Party
at Dracula's' for this little knees-up.**

Unpacking the Hamper

This lot all had dinner at Liberace's last night. Liberace put a lot of Champagne away and is paying the price now. Poor Sammy went back to Frank's, made a phone call, and still hasn't been to bed. Mae's sitting pretty; she doesn't drink.

Sammy's career successes were extraordinary: #1 records, TV programmes, Broadway shows and years and years of Vegas residencies. There was much dedicated, heavy drinking along the way, and later on, a great deal of other business, too. As Sammy once said 'if you get the title of Swinger, you can't sit in the library all day.'

God bless Scott Thorson – after their smoothies this morning he made Liberace a vat of chicken soup, which he is supping now from a nifty little tub. Sammy, also a fan of a liquid lunch, fancies a milkshake. Mae loves milkshakes and ask Scott to stop at the drive-thru they're passing.

Mae does what they do in Japan and gets a plain McFlurry with a large fries on the side for dunking. 'Sweet and salty,' she says. 'Sounds weird, but think of a burger and a milkshake.'

Liberace's sticking with his soup, thank you – he finds fast food crass. Being a gent though, he gets Scott's usual nuggets, saying 'I hope you still got those sauce sachets and Tabasco in the glovebox!'

Alas, Sammy's run out of cigarettes! Scott pulls over at the liquor store and Sammy dashes in. He comes back with them and a miniature bourbon and vodka. Liberace sticks the vodka in the end of his soup. 'Taa daa – just like that, my lunch becomes a nourishing beverage!'

'Same here,' Sammy says, tipping the bourbon into his milkshake.

Pack your own

Where do you get chicken soup this good if you don't make it? Please make it. The smell in your house alone is worth it. And I'm sure you know where to go to get a milkshake and fries ...

Chicken Soup

For a soup with such renowned healing properties, this is simple enough to make, as most things just go in the pot.

Serves 4 hungry people

1 x 1.5–2 kg (3 lb 7 oz–4 lb 7 oz)
   whole organic chicken
2 onions, peeled and quartered
2 carrots, peeled and roughly chopped
3 celery stalks, roughly chopped
2 bay leaves
5 sprigs of parsley

1 teaspoon salt
¼ teaspoon white pepper

To serve
1 carrot, finely sliced into rounds
   (optional)

Put the chicken, onions, carrots and celery into a large stockpot or saucepan and add enough water to cover the chicken by about 2.5 cm (1 in). Bring to the boil, then let it bubble gently, uncovered, for 20 minutes, skimming off any froth or scum as it forms. Turn the heat down to low and add the bay leaves, parsley, salt and pepper, then cover and simmer slowly for an hour.

Remove the chicken from the soup and pick the meat from the carcass. Keep the chicken meat to one side, then return the carcass to the pot and simmer for another hour.

Strain the soup through a sieve lined with a clean tea towel into a clean saucepan – this will help to filter out any impurities and some of the fat. Put the pan of soup over a low heat, add the chicken meat and, if you like, the sliced carrot. Check the seasoning and adjust with salt and pepper to taste.

When the carrots are merrily bobbing at the surface of the hot soup, you are ready to serve. Ladle the soup into bowls and eat.

Pickle-y Fries

That's right, fast-food-style fries at home. I would only do this if you aren't within striking distance of a well-regarded, fast-food chain or if you're having a dinner party or something. It is undeniably a lot of work for a chip, but worth it if the occasion is right or you just like cooking. You'll need to plan ahead, as the potatoes need a nice soak in brine.

Makes enough for 4 people

600 g (1 lb 5 oz) russet potatoes
2 litres (70 fl oz/8 cups) rapeseed
   (canola) oil, for deep-frying

For the brine
225 g (8 oz) salt
225 g (8 oz) soft brown sugar
200 ml (7 fl oz/scant 1 cup) white
   wine vinegar

Start by making your brine. Pour 2 litres (70 fl oz/8 cups) of water into a pan and add the salt, sugar and vinegar. Place over a high heat and stir until the salt and sugar have dissolved – do not let it boil. Pour the brine into a large heatproof container and leave to one side to cool.

Meanwhile, peel the potatoes and place in a bowl of cold water. Remove the potatoes, one by one, and cut them first into 5 mm (¼ in) slices, then stack those slices and cut them into 5 mm (¼ in) matchsticks. Drop the chips into the cooled brine and leave for at least 4 hours, or overnight.

When you're ready to cook, drain the chips and rinse well in a couple of changes of cold water. Spread them out on paper towels and pat dry.

Pour enough oil for deep-frying into a deep-fryer or a large, heavy-based saucepan and heat to 150°C (300°F). Working in batches, carefully lower your chips into the hot oil, without overcrowding them. Leave to blanch for 5 minutes before removing and draining on paper towels. The chips will be very soft at this stage, and that is fine.

Once all the chips are blanched, heat the oil to 200°C (400°F) and, again in batches, fry the chips for a couple of minutes until golden brown. Drain on yet more paper towels and immediately hit the chips with a dusting of salt.

Voilà! Dunk them in your milkshake and congratulate yourself.

Bourbon Milkshake

Ben and I genuinely think milkshakes are one of the most delicious things in the world. Does everyone think that? I particularly like them when they've got booze in.

Makes 4 milkshakes

450 g (1 lb) vanilla ice cream, plus more if needed

350 ml (1½ cups/12 fl oz) whole milk
175 ml (6 fl oz/¾ cup) bourbon

Place four big glasses in the freezer to chill while you make the milkshake.

Put the ice cream, milk and bourbon into a powerful blender and blitz like a banshee until smooth.

Remove those frosty glasses from the freezer and pour in the milkshake. Find a straw and suck, suck, suck it up.

$$HACKS$$

Six picnicker's cocktails made with booze miniatures

1 **Bloody Hell Mary:**
gin or vodka added to
leftover gazpacho (page
138) or shop-bought
tomato soup.

2 **The Wake and Shake: rum,**
Amaretto or Baileys added
to milkshakes – works a
dream whether they're
from a fast-food chain or
store-bought.

3 **A Park Bench Pina Colada:**
white rum, Malibu and
a dash of coconut milk,
cut with pineapple juice
(pour the rest of the
coconut milk over some
tinned or fresh fruit if
it tickles your fancy).

4 **Sgroppino Bambino:**
a big scoop of lemon
sorbet ('a cup, not a cone,
please'), a splash from
a mini prosecco bottle and
half a vodka miniature, all
beaten into submission/
slushie heaven…

5 **So Nearly Sangria: mini**
red wine bottle and a can
of Sprite … plus a brandy
miniature if you've got one.

6 **Running the Gimlet: Jif**
lime juice squeezed into
a miniature of gin and
DOWNED. Hahahaha.

A Surrealist Picn'

Cold outside? No kind of atmosphere? Have another ladle of the poached coffee pig's fish fingers, imagine you're inside and get on with the party.

Undeniably uber-talented as a group (the works of Magritte and Dalí are nothing short of sublime), the Surrealists did and said A LOT of really weird stuff and, as individuals. Imagine being one of the finest painters ever to have lived, and deciding that you need to walk about with an anteater on a lead to attract attention – Salvador, we're looking at you. Say what you like about Picasso, but you never saw him in a novelty hat. As well as a painter, Dali was a commercial genius. He painted the greatest crucifixion of the 20th Century (Crucifixion (Corpus Hypercubus), designed perfume and brandy bottles, advertised Alka Seltzer and unbeknown to most, designed the Chupa Chups logo in 1969.

Of all the theoretically fascinating people at our fantasy picnic, Lee Miller was the real deal. One night, at the age of nineteen, she walked out of her brownstone apartment on Manhattan's West 48th Street straight into oncoming traffic, but was plucked from the road by a passer-by. Her rescuer turned out to be legendary publisher Condé Nast, and within two years she had appeared on the cover of *Vogue* and was an enormously successful model. It wouldn't be long, though, before she decided she wanted to 'take photographs, not be in them'. Upping sticks, she moved to Paris and promptly ensconced herself as muse, lover and collaborator of the great Surrealist and photographer Man Ray.

MENU

Meat Trifle

Roast Cauliflower with Herbed Couscous

Campari, Crème de Menthe and Orange Ice Lollies

Liquid Sunshine

Fantasy Host
Lee Miller

Fantasy Guests
Roland Penrose, Meret Oppenheim, Salvador Dalí, André Breton, Max Ernst, Man Ray, René Magritte

Location
Meret Oppenheim's garden in Switzerland

Dress Code
Stupid hats and velvet suits, fur bracelets and sugar-cube rings à la Meret Oppenheim

Unpacking the Hamper

Lee Miller married Roland Penrose in 1947 and settled at Farleys House, in Sussex. There they threw LEGENDARY dinner parties, with guests including Picasso, Miró and Max Ernst. During the feasts there would be flashes of the old Surrealist in her – green chicken and blue spaghetti – but most importantly there was much errant deliciousness, and it is this ethos that our picnic is based on. Remember, despite the guff that often surrounds it, food and cooking aren't about looking clever, making a statement or striving to be arty and original, they are about deliciousness.

Our gang's spread is laid out on a few of Meret Oppenheim's famous bird-leg tables in the garden, of her house in Switzerland, the air is clear and crisp and beautiful and filled with a palpable carefree enjoyment.

In her invite, Lee told everyone to bring something to eat that looks like one thing but is really another – JAZZ HANDS CRAZY Hahahah!

Dalí has rocked up with a savoury trifle that he is EXTREMELY pleased with and is busy telling Miller about: 'There's shredded braised beef, set in its jellied cooking liquor, a layer of chicken liver pâté on top of that, then boulangère potatoes, and finally horseradish crème fraîche'.

The whole thing looks like a giant B-52 shooter from a student union in the 90s. She's so impressed she tells Dalí he should do a cookbook, which he tells her he already has.

Max Ernst and René Magritte arrive together, with a bowl of rice that they insist isn't a bowl of rice – Sigh.

Meret Oppenheim's gone all out and made a cake resembling her sculpture *Ma Gouvernante*, which was composed of a pair of high heels trussed together to look like roasted meat.

The real star, though, is Lee Miller herself. She has recreated one of her most famous show-stopper dishes from those heady days at Farleys: a massive pair of roasted cauliflowers. Don't ask about Man Ray and André Breton! Taking dull to new levels, they have distanced themselves from the group and are sitting on a separate balcony reading existential poetry to each other.

At my Sandwich Shop on a Sunday, everything kicks off with pints of Campari and orange juice, one of life's great joys. What a beverage – it tastes like grown-up ice lollies AND gets you drunk! On family holidays when my sister Lydia and I were little, our dad used to have it at breakfast. He'd gleefully stir his glass until the two sunset-y liquids merged into a uniform, beautiful blood-orange colour. Leaning to my sister and I, he would whisper, 'People think you're drinking grapefruit juice.'

Miller loves the idea of the drink so much she's decided to turn it into ice lollies for everyone and is calling them Liquid Sunshine, which is a funny thing to do as it is snowing here in Switzerland.

Pack your own

I'm not sure whether you'd actually want to make and eat Dalí's Meat Trifle as a whole thing, but the individual components are all useful culinary arrows to have in your quiver, and delicious in their own right.

Lee Miller is probably the one to pay attention to here! The lollies are gorgeous and portable in an ice-cube-filled Thermos, and as long as you leave the cherries and peas off the cauliflowers, they are rather nice, too.

Six wonderful things to mix into mayonnaise

Start with a couple of tablespoons of mayo and about the same
of the other ingredient/s, then taste – you can always add more
mayo … Use your supercharged mayo in sandwiches and salads,
or for dunking raw vegetables or slivers of toast.

1   Leftover gravy: I've said
    it before and I'll say it again
    – heat up your gravy and it
    will mix in like a dream.

2   Tarragon: go heavy and
    blend it up with some
    vegetable oil if you can be
    bothered; otherwise, just
    pick the leaves and chop
    them mad-fine – tarragon
    mayo is amazing with
    steak, and I love it with
    pretty much anything.

3   Leftover bolognese (or
    ragù, or 'nduja): heat it up
    and mix it in – NAUGHTY,
    NAUGHTY, NAUGHTY.

4   Garlic, orange and green
    olive tapenade: finely grate
    one or two garlic cloves,
    sprinkle with salt and
    smoosh with the flat of
    a knife until you get garlic
    goo; squeeze the juice
    of an orange into a small
    saucepan and boil until

thick and sticky. Open
the jar of tapenade and
stir a couple of tablepoons
into mayo, along with
your garlic goo and orange
syrup. You can thank
me later.

5   Serious quantities of
    the fat and juices from
    a roast chicken: heat it up
    and mix like a bastard –
    you'll be surprised how
    much you can get into a few
    tablespoons of Hellmann's.
    Chicken sandwiches of
    the gods approaching…

6   Yoghurt, honey and
    balsamic vinegar: oh,
    my gosh, but this makes
    an amazing dressing for
    salads, leftover roast
    chicken – and leftover
    roast chicken salads,
    of course!

Meat Trifle

This is most certainly a project cook. All told, you'll need the best part of a week for shopping, prep and cooking here. Is it worth it? Probably not. Unless, like Dalí, you think the eventual spectacle is worth the toil. One piece of good news: each element of this recipe is a bona fide banger, so if you don't make the whole trifle, do try one or two bits from it in isolation.

2.5 kg (5 lb 10 oz) beef short ribs
1 tablespoon salt
1 tablespoon freshly ground
   black pepper
1 tablespoon rapeseed (canola) oil
2 onions, roughly chopped
2 x 400 g (14oz) tins of plum tomatoes
1 head of garlic, cloves separated
   and peeled
750 ml (25 fl oz/3 cups) red wine
1 quantity of chicken liver pâté
   (page 80)
75 g (2½ oz) toasted hazelnuts, chopped
Finely grated zest of 1 lemon

For the boulangère potatoes
100 g (3½ oz) butter
2 onions, finely sliced
2 garlic cloves, finely chopped
2 sprigs of rosemary, leaves picked
   and chopped
Large pinch of salt
4 large potatoes, weighing about 1 kg
   (2 lb 4 oz) in total
100 ml (3½ fl oz) chicken stock

For the horseradish crème fraîche
150 ml (5 fl oz) creamed horseradish
150 ml (5 fl oz) crème fraîche
150 ml (5 fl oz) double (heavy) cream
Juice of 1 lemon

Season your short ribs with the salt and pepper – the amounts may seem excessive, but you are effectively seasoning the whole dish, not just the meat. Place a large, heavy-based saucepan over a high heat and add the oil. Once the oil is hot, add the ribs and sear for 3 minutes on each side, until they have formed a dark crust. Add the chopped onions and the tinned tomatoes and scrape around the pan to deglaze any tasty bits that have caramelised on the pan. Add the garlic, stir to combine, then pour in the wine and bring to the boil. Immediately reduce the heat, cover and leave the ribs blipping away over a low heat for 2½–3 hours. They are ready when the meat pulls easily away from the bone. Set aside until cool enough to handle, then remove the bones and shred the meat. Transfer the beef, with all its sauce, to the fridge, so you get a nice jelly when the liquor cools.

Meanwhile, crack on with the boulangère potatoes. Preheat your oven to 200°C (400°F/gas 7). Melt half the butter in a large casserole or ovenproof saucepan, and when it is foaming, add the sliced onions, garlic, rosemary and salt and sauté until soft and golden brown. While they are cooking, peel the potatoes and slice them super-thinly (ideally with a mandoline). When the onions are ready, take the pan off the heat and use a slotted spoon to remove half of them from the pan. Add half of the potatoes to the pan in a nicely overlapped single layer, then put back the onions you've just removed, followed by the other half of the potatoes, again taking care to keep them in a nice layer. Dot with the remaining butter and pour over the chicken stock, giving the pan a shake to spread the stock evenly around the potatoes. Transfer to the oven and cook for 20–30 minutes until the potatoes are golden brown on top and a knife goes through them easily. Leave to one side to cool.

I am sure you've had time to make the horseradish crème fraîche by now. This is no more difficult than mixing everything together.

So, finally, it's time to assemble the trifle. Find a trifle dish, aka a large glass bowl or similar, and start by pushing your cold beef, with all its jelly, into the base. On top of this place a layer of half the boulangère potatoes, then the chicken liver pâté, followed by the rest of the potatoes. Spread over the horseradish crème fraîche.

You are now that proud owner of a savoury trifle Dalí would be proud of. Take it and unveil it at a picnic, receive the plaudits willingly, ensure everyone has a little try and then humbly accept the surprised praise. Do not, though, tell them how long it took you to make. They will laugh in your face.

Roast Cauliflower with Herbed Couscous

Leave the cherries and peas off this and it's actually rather nice.

Makes enough for 4

2 medium cauliflowers
2 tablespoons ras el hanout
2 tablespoons tomato purée (paste)
2 teaspoons chilli powder
1 tablespoon red wine vinegar
4 tablespoons olive oil
200 g (7 oz) couscous
1 bunch of parsley, leaves picked and
   finely chopped

1 bunch of dill, leaves picked and
   finely chopped
1 bunch of mint, leaves picked and
   finely chopped
Juice of 1 lemon
2 glacé cherries
2 peas
Salt

Preheat your oven to 200°C (400°F/gas 7) and find a roasting tray large enough to hold the two cauliflowers. Pop the whole cauliflowers into a large bowl and add the ras el hanout, tomato purée, chilli powder, vinegar, oil and two good pinches of salt and rub vigorously all over.

Place the two spiced orbs, flat side down, side by side in the tray and roast in the oven for 35–40 minutes, until nice and golden brown. Test their doneness with a small knife or skewer, which should slide easily in and out of the thickest part of the cauliflower – any resistance encountered should be met head on with a further 10 minutes in the oven before checking again.

While the cauliflower is cooking, put the couscous into a large heatproof bowl and season with a pinch of salt. Put 3 tablespoons of the olive oil and the lemon juice into 200 ml (7 fl oz/scant 1 cup) of boiling water, mix it all about and pour over the couscous and cover the bowl with cling film (plastic wrap) and leave for 15 minutes. Fluff the couscous up with a fork and stir the herbs through it. Spoon the couscous onto a serving platter and place the cauliflowers side by side on top. Sit a cherry on top of each cauliflower and put a pea on top of those. Hold them in place with a cocktail stick.

Deliver to the picnic venue and wait to see how long it is until someone remarks on your witty little creation.

Campari, Crème de Menthe and Orange Ice Lollies

The absolute truth is that I might prefer these lollies without the crème de menthe. I can't decide. Please let me know what you think! You'll need lolly moulds for this. If you haven't got any sack this off completely, get yourself a fruit ice lolly and mix a glass of Campari and Orange to go on the side.

Makes 6 lollies

600 ml (20 fl oz/2½ cups) freshly squeezed orange juice
Zest of 1 orange

100 g (3½ oz) caster (superfine) sugar
3 tablespoons Campari
3 tablespoons crème de menthe

Heat the orange juice, zest and sugar in a heavy-based saucepan over a medium heat. Stir to help dissolve the sugar, but do not let it boil. Once the sugar has dissolved, remove from the heat and allow to cool.

Divide the orange juice into three equal parts. Add the Campari to one part and the crème de menthe to another, leaving the final part as it is. Now distribute the plain orange juice evenly between six lolly moulds and place in the freezer. Give it an hour or two to freeze solid, then add the Campari mix and freeze for another hour or two. Finally, add the crème de menthe layer and return to the freezer for several hours until completely frozen.

To release the lollies from their moulds, very briefly hold the base of the moulds under warm running water.

The Fast-Food Pic Are Made Of

McDonald's, helping us picnic like BOSSES since 1940.

In his brilliant book *McDonald's: Behind the Arches*, John F. Love tells the story of how McDonald's took over the world. We learn about the fascinating battle between Ray Kroc, who went on to own the business, and the McDonald's brothers, who started it. As the Henry Fords of hamburgers, the McDonald brothers' ideas about how food could be put together gave Ray Kroc the structure for a business that, by 2019, had so many restaurants it fed just under one per cent of the global population on a daily basis.

At the beginning of the film *The Founder*, in which Ray Kroc is portrayed by Michael Keaton, there is a wonderful moment. Queuing outside at the first McDonald's in San Bernardino, Keaton gets to the front and places his order. The food comes so fast he cannot believe it is his. It is all wrapped up and neatly popped in a bag, rather than being on a tray with cutlery etc as he was expecting. Blown away by the efficiency of the system, he loses himself a little and asks the grinning geezer serving him where he should eat it. The guy gives him a kindly look, and says: 'Your car? At the park? At home? Wherever you like!'

McDonald's, helping us picnic like a BOSS, since 1940.

One look at how picnics are portrayed and you'd think they belonged to Jane Austen or Fortnum & Mason! They don't though, do they? McDonald's owns the picnic – we just never noticed. Think about where you've eaten a McDonald's – in the back of cars, trains, airport waiting areas, motorway lay-bys, on coaches, in tents, sitting on walls, at the back of car parks, at home, everywhere! We've been picnicking on McDonald's since we were kids.

Ben's Infinitely Hackable Sausage and Egg Muffin

The Big Max

Chicken Kiev Parmo

Lagerita-Shandy

Fantasy Host
Me. It's my birthday, innit!

Fantasy Guests
You lot!

Location
Anywhere you've brought something to eat that could be looked at a little differently, pimped up and enjoyed all the more.

Dress Code
Fancy dress!! And the more ridiculous, the better – they'll love you down the drive-thru.

Unpacking the Hamper

Unlike all the other picnics in this book, this one isn't a fantasy. It is a recreation of my 36th birthday party. I love my birthday and always try to do something that is, as my mum would say, a hoot.

Nineteen guests were told to be at the baseball field in Finsbury Park, North London, in fancy dress, by 10 a.m. and to bring their favourite condiment and eight miniature bottles of spirits – a WhatsApp Group helped to ensure a good mix of spirits and not too many duplicates on the condiment front.

On arrival, everyone was given a cheat sheet of McDonald's hacks and asked to think about what sounded great or how they might freestyle independently. At 10.15 a.m., a group of cabs arrived on cue and, like a gang of out-of-shape Mardi Gras dancers, we headed for one of London's legendary drive-thrus, the 24-hour McDonald's on Green Lanes in Harringay.

My timing was immaculate. As the convoy pulled into the car park, someone in my cab said, 'Hang on, it's 10.25 a.m., do we all have to have breakfast?' I hopped out and told the first cab to go through and load up on hash browns, sausage and egg McMuffins, twenty double espressos and all the other good breakfast stuff. The rest of us, in the other three cabs, would swoop through moments later and order from the daytime menu.

We got back to the park and prepared diligently for the encroaching munchies. I'd brought a load of old instant ramen noodle flavour packs from the Sandwich Shop, which were an unexpected touch on fries, McNuggets, chicken selects and the like. Some people brought vinegar which was a brilliant idea. A few drops of Forum Chardonnay Vinegar in a milkshake? A REVELATION! With thirsts raging, we made a start on the assembled miniatures.

Fernet-Branca went into Coke, Campari into Fanta and Tropicana mixed together; gin found its way into Sprite, as did Cointreau and tequila, topped up with a beer someone had brought, making a kind of lagerita that became our drink of the summer that year.

Pudding dawned. People crushed apple pies into McFlurries, others mixed Neapolitan milkshakes from a third each of strawberry, vanilla and chocolate. Baileys and Malibu in a vanilla milkshake, and brandy and Kahlua in a chocolate one were both to die for. And all the milkshakes were improved by the Horlicks my girlfriend had brought for 'malting'.

I made a chicken parmo sandwich by loading up a McChicken sandwich with three mozzarella dippers and their whole tub of salsa but the idea of the day was definitely the McDonald's Irish coffee: 1 x vanilla milkshake, a few drops of posh vinegar, a McDonald's double espresso and two miniature bottles of Jameson's … STIR STIR STIR, BOOM BOOM BOOM!

In America and Australia, you have a WAY bigger food and drink selection at McDonald's than we have in the UK, so I'd LOVE to know what mad stuff you come up with: please message me @lunchluncheon to tell me what you've done!!!

Pack your own

Unlike me, you might not be moronically loyal to merely one fast-food outlet. Whether you're into KFC, Popeyes, Wendy's, or even bloody Burger King, come up with your own hacks – they're the pot of gold at the end of the rainbow. Whatever you do, please promise me one thing: use your chosen fast-food outlet as a picnicking springboard. Buy from their menu, smash items together – fill your pockets with their sachets, sauces and napkins, then head out into the world and picnic like your life depends on it.

HACKS

Six super-lush quick-pickles to make in the brine left in a just-finished jar of dill pickles

Remember, NEVER put your fingers in the pickle jar – use a fork or some tongs to get everything out and put everything in. Most of these things will be ready enough in a few hours, but give them a few days in the fridge to really get to know their pickle-y side:

1 Quail's eggs: boil for 3.5 minutes, then submerge in cold water. Peel them gently, still in the water, starting at the tip and moving round and down concentrically. These are particularly fun popped into a finished jar of pickled beetroot.

2 Hotdogs (nice posh kielbasa or kabanos, or cheapo franks).

3 A mix of halved grapes, nectarine quarters and whole cherries (mind your teeth on those cherry stones – or pit them on entry). These are great in salads.

4 Pomegranate seeds: again in salads or stirred through rich meat dishes at the end of the cooking

5 Fennel seeds: these are magic in a fennel salad. If you cut a fennel bulb as thinly as you can (or risk a mandolin injury), then soak it in ice-cold water, the fennel will curl up beautifully and go very crisp.

6 Topped and tailed green beans – an American classic!!!

Ben's Infinitely Hackable Sausage and Egg Muffin

It can be a right pest when you rise too late for the greatest sandwich of all time from the lads with the golden arches. So worry ye not, you can now make it at home. While this recipe makes two muffins and, as such, could be construed as a recipe for two people, the reality is you will want to eat both of these, so double up if you're dining with a friend.

Makes 2

2 high-quality plain pork sausages
1–2 tablespoons olive oil
2 medium free-range eggs

4 cheese slices (ideally American cheese)
2 English muffins

Take your sausages, slice down their length and remove the skin then shape the sausagemeat into two round patties of equal size; these won't need any additional seasoning.

Place a large frying pan over a high heat and add a splash of oil. When the oil is hot, add your sausage patties to the pan and leave them to cook undisturbed for 2 minutes. Flip the patties and give them a further 2 minutes. They should be a nice golden brown on both sides.

In the same pan (if you have room), crack the eggs into the oil in the pan – you may need to add a splash more – and use a spatula to shape them into rough circles about the same size as the patties. When the whites are nearly cooked through, flip the eggs over to seal both sides.

Carefully lift the eggs onto the patties, lay 2 cheese slices over each one and cover with the lid or a large heatproof bowl to allow the cheese to melt in the steam – this should only take 20 seconds.

Slice the muffins in half and briefly press them, cut-side down, into the pan to toast in the porky oil.

Building your sausage and egg muffin is as simple as base, patty, top. Give it a squeeze to break the yolk, condiment and hack at your leisure and GO GO GO.

The Big Max

The hardest thing here is the sauce, and that is a cinch, so you're in for an easy ride.

Makes 1 massive burger

150 g (5 oz) minced (ground) beef
1 tablespoon olive oil
1 sesame seed burger bun
¼ onion, very finely chopped
¼ head iceberg lettuce, finely shredded
2 cheese slices (ideally American
   burger cheese)
1 large dill pickle, thinly sliced
Salt and freshly ground black pepper

**For the sauce – makes enough
   for 4 burgers**
100 g (4 oz/ ½ cup) mayonnaise
   (Hellmann's is the daddy)
50 g (2oz/ ¼ cup) Sweet Pickle Relish
   (If you can't buy this, grate a big dill
   pickle and mix it with ½ a teaspoon
   of caster (superfine) sugar)
1 teaspoon white wine vinegar
2 tablespoons French's mustard
1 teaspoon onion powder
1 teaspoon garlic powder
1 teaspoon paprika (not smoked)

Start by combining all the sauce ingredients in a bowl and mixing well. Leave to one side while you make the burger.

Season the meat with salt and pepper and form into two balls of equal size. Heat the oil in a frying pan over a high heat. Place the patties in the pan and immediately smash them flat with the back of a spatula – be firm. Leave the patties to cook without moving them for 2 minutes each side, or until nice and dark and crispy.

Meanwhile, slice each burger bun into three sections. These are known in the trade as the heel (base), the club (middle) and the crown (top). Lightly toast the club on both sides and the heel and crown on the inside only.

To assemble the burgers, spread a little sauce over the heel and the club, then top with some chopped onion and lettuce. Lay the cheese slices on the heel and some pickles on the club, followed by a patty on each. Lift the club onto the heel, then top with the crown.

Admire your genius and take a big bite.

Chicken Kiev Parmo

This is some pretty remarkable alchemy. God bless the good people of Middlesbrough – we hope they won't mind the shake-up of using kievs and swapping the béchamel for tomato passata. We promise it's banging.

Makes 2

2 ready-made chicken Kievs
4 tablespoons tomato passata
(sieved tomatoes)

1 ball of mozzarella, cut into rounds
2 relatively robust white burger buns
(sesame or poppy seeds optional)

Preheat the oven to 180°C (350°F/gas 4) and line a baking tray (pan) with baking parchment.

Place the chicken Kievs on the baking tray and cook in the oven for 20 minutes (or as per the instructions on the pack)?.

When ready, remove from the oven and turn on your grill (broiler) to its highest setting.

Top the chicken Kievs with the tomato passata, then the mozzarella, covering as much of the Kiev as possible. Cook under the grill for 2–3 minutes until the mozzarella is blistering and browned. Transfer your parmo Kievs to a board or plate and leave to cool slightly while you cut your buns in half and toast the cut sides under the grill.

Lift your parmo Kievs onto the bases of the buns, pop the lids on top and give them a squish. I always cut mine in half, and let some of the goodness come out on to the plate for dunking in! Or you could, being careful not to burn yourself, take a massive mouthful and let the garlicky, buttery filling run down your chin – mind your new sneakers though – this one's a dripper!

A Picnic at Max's

Born in Haggerston (then outside London) in 1656, Edmond Halley was part of a small group of scientists and thinkers who changed our understanding of the world. He was one of the people Isaac Newton was talking about when he said: 'If I have seen further, it is by standing on the shoulders of giants.' Newton was also having a pop at the stature of one of the people he hated the most, inventor of the microscope, Robert Hooke.

As my great-great-great-whatever Granddad, Edmond Halley is of mythical importance in my life. Being related to someone with a celestial body named after them is a peculiar privilege of which I am extremely proud, but it hasn't always smelled of roses. It was particularly crushing at 15, when I broke the family tradition of scientific endeavour and failed my maths exams. He must have spun in his grave.

As ancient relatives go, he is easy to imagine: what with the comet, the books and all the paintings and stuff, I feel I know him somehow, even though he's been dead for 280 years. He pushed for, and paid for, the publication of his friend Newton's *Principia Mathematica*, figured out the data analysis behind life insurance, reconfigured the diving bell, made the world's first meteorological charts and a plethora of other extraordinary things.

As his descendant, my dad, Ned Halley, might not have done anything quite so revolutionary BUT I'd like to share with you all something he has figured out about the world. And it involves breakfast. And happiness.

Despite all our ancestor's accolades, I'm every bit as proud of my Dad's discovery as anything The Big Lebowski did. Breakfast and happiness aren't about what direction winds travel the earth, how rocks swing round the sun or breathing underwater, but they are, and we all know it, what makes the world go round.

Born in Brazil to a Brazilian mother and a German father in 1940, Astrud Gilberto put the BOSS in bossa nova, and my love for her runs deeper than just her lackadaisical delivery, beautiful voice and hatred of interviews. Her 1965 album, creatively titled *The Astrud Gilberto Album*, has soundtracked breakfast at my parent's house EVERY Saturday they have ever been at home, for 45 years and counting. Despite only listening to the record once a week, it has theme-tuned the consumption of croissants, coffee, and tea nearly 2,400 times.

The second time you wake up at my mum and dad's house (known as The Mousehole) on a Saturday morning, you realise it isn't just the music that's familiar. Everything happening is part of their routine. Round and round and round, a steady, violent whirring like Sweeney Todd's meat grinder floats down the corridor as you stir in your bed. It's my mum, going hell for leather on her hand-powered coffee grinder. Round and round and round.

By 9:15 a.m. my dad's been down town and got milk, bought the Saturday papers and three croissants, one and a half each for him and my mum, every week the same. When he got home the croissants went straight in the oven, covered in foil, to heat up all nice. Coffee and tea are brewing. I know what cups they will drink from, what jug the milk for my dad's tea will be in and which butter dish will be on the table. I even know which sections of the newspaper they will read first...

If you are less like my dad and more like me, you don't want to go down the shops on Saturday morning, so stock up on Friday and those pyjamas can stay exactly where they are. Treat yourself too, if you like hot chocolate buy a really posh one, you only use a tiny bit every week.

The sheer reliability, and my familiarity with, the goings on in this small piece of Somerset at 9:30 a.m. on a Saturday, tethers me completely.

My Mum's Lasagne

Three Toasted Croissants to Beat All Toasted Croissants

The World's Best Hot Chocolate

Fantasy Host
Edmond Halley

Fantasy Guest
Astrud Gilberto

Location
Maybe it's the park, or your garden, or a field. Somewhere close by, so those toasted croissants are still warm; somewhere you can see the world and how busy it all is, while you sit calmly, enjoying your savoury pastries and chocolate milk...

Dress Code
Massive, curly white wigs and your favourite, comfy, loungewear.

Unpacking the Hamper

Even if Saturday mornings are out, there's bound to be a time in the week when you can eat and drink something you really love. A moment when you can put your favourite socks on, play THAT Bon Jovi album and let the good times roll as you stare calmly from the window at the busy world outside. Give it a go, every week for a month – make a routine, same time, same place, same stuff. As my Dad says: 'It's an underestimated pleasure, having something to look forward to that much, that happens every week.'

I haven't copied my parents' routines, but I've made plenty of my own. I have tried to litter my life with them. For me, repetition, routine and continuity bring great comfort. Most of mine involve food, keep me on the emotional straight and narrow and are both affordable and achievable luxuries.

For years, my sister Lydia and I have got together once a month or so, to have roast chicken, rice, and coleslaw. I cook it every time. We always have supermarket coleslaw and it's my Death Row Meal. A culinary Holy Trinity. Father, Son and Holy Shredded Vegetables Covered in Mayonnaise. Amen.

In her very Scandinavian manner, my mum told me when I was about 18 that I was never to forget how lucky I am to have been born stupid enough to wake up every day thinking everything will be alright.

My dear mama was in hospital for a few weeks at the beginning of 2020 (and has thankfully since emerged, all guns blazing). My dad and I were together at home for a surreal Saturday Breakfast, the first one ever without her. I sat where I would usually sit, facing into the room, and my dad said, 'Why don't you come round here and sit in your mum's seat?' It felt weird, but he said, 'Come on, sit round here. She sits there so she can see into the garden and watch the birds.' The penny dropped. None of the things they do are habits for habits' sake. They have looked at what makes them happy and sought to find those things in simple, achievable ways. They have taken the dullest of tasks, we all must partake in, like breakfast, and turned it into a joy. Sat there, with my poor ma in hospital, I had never been more inspired by her way of seeing the world.

As a #lasagnelifer, I make lasagne at least once a month – and I ALWAYS make extra béchamel. I try and have it on a Thursday or Friday, so that on Saturday morning, I can revel in thoughts of my parents and their Puritan croissants while I – Astrud on of course – stuff a croissant with ham, cheese and béchamel and grill it in my sandwich toastie machine. I have even been known to put a slice of leftover lasagne in a croissant and grill that. PICNICKING LIKE A BOSS.

Pack your own

I'm loath to say anything about what you might want in your routine. The things that make us feel happy and snug, and serve to rekindle fond memories are, of course, highly personal. I will, though, make a plea: never forget, anything can go in a croissant, especially toasted – and toasted croissants really do travel well, as does hot chocolate.

PLEASE message me @lunchluncheon to tell me if you've made a routine for yourself and, if so, what it is! Or just to tell me that you have no time for any of this bullshit in your life, you think I'm a soppy wanker who's completely missed the mark here and, quite frankly, you were hoping for more from this stupid book about picnics.

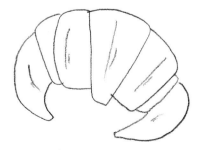

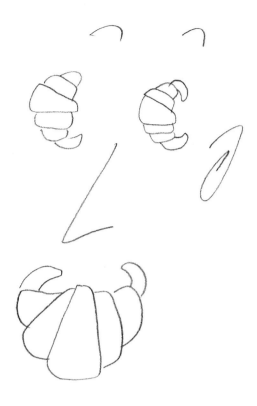

THREE TOASTED CROISSANTS
TO BEAT ALL TOASTED CROISSANTS

Each recipe below is for one, but it shouldn't take Carol Vorderman to multiply up the amounts for however many croissants you need to make.

Ham, Cheddar, Mustard and Leftover Béchamel

1 croissant (a day old is fine)
1 tablespoon leftover béchamel
2 slices thick-cut ham

50 g (2 oz) mature Cheddar, grated
Dijon mustard, to taste

Spread each half with a layer of béchamel, then put a slice of ham on the bottom, smear it with mustard, cheese on top of that, other slice of ham on top of that and put the lid on.

Either pop the croissant in your toastie machine or put a heavy-based frying pan over a low-medium heat. You want to grill/toast the croissant slowly with a weight on top of it so that the inside melts completely before the outside burns. When the bottom is looking lovely and tempting, turn the croissant over and repeat.

Remove from the pan and allow to cool for a few minutes before taking a massive bite.

Nduja or Chorizo, Taleggio and Honey

1 croissant (a day old is fine)
30 g (1 oz) nduja or chorizo

4 thick slices Taleggio
2 teaspoons honey

Use a serrated knife to open up your croissant.

Spread the 'nduja (or lay the chorizo) over the inside bottom half of the croissant and put the Taleggio on top. Close the lid.

Either pop the croissant in your toastie machine or put a heavy-based frying pan over a low-medium heat. You want to grill/toast the croissant slowly with a weight on top of it so that the inside melts completely before the outside burns. When the bottom is looking lovely and tempting, turn the croissant over and repeat.

Remove from the pan and allow to cool for a few minutes before drizzling with honey, getting it down you and probably making another one.

Mascarpone, Almond Butter, Lemon Curd and Toasted Almonds

1 croissant (a day old is fine)
2 tablespoons mascarpone
1 tablespoon almond butter

1 tablespoon lemon curd
25 g (1 oz) flaked almonds, toasted
in a dry frying pan

Use a serrated knife to open up your croissant.

Spread a layer of mascarpone on each half of the croissant, followed by dollops of almond butter and lemon curd.

Scatter over the toasted almonds, then close the lid.

Either pop the croissant in your toastie machine or put a heavy-based frying pan over a low-medium heat. You want to grill/toast the croissant slowly with a weight on top of it so that the inside melts completely before the outside burns. When the bottom is looking lovely and tempting, turn the croissant over and repeat.

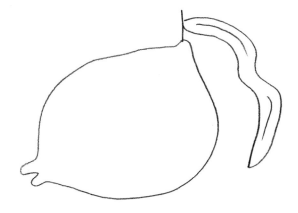

The World's Best Hot Chocolate

To be quite frank, it's hard to beat a tablespoon of hot chocolate powder, some hot milk, a squirt of cream from a can and a dusting of cocoa. If you do want to step it up a gear though, why not try a hot chocolate made of genuine chocolate?

Makes 1 indulgent hot chocolate
– double or triple to your heart's content

250 ml (8½ fl oz/1 cup) whole milk
40 g (1½ oz) dark chocolate, finely chopped or grated

20 g (¾ oz) milk chocolate, finely chopped or grated
Pinch of salt
2 tablespoons single (light) cream

Heat half the milk in a pan over a medium heat and add the chocolate. Stir until the chocolate has fully melted, then whisk in the remaining milk. Continue to heat the mixture until steaming but not boiling. Remove from the heat and add the salt, then the cream, giving it one final frantic whisk to get a little layer of bubbles, then serve.

My Mum's Lasagne

My mum uses Robert Carrier's for the Bolognese.

Serves 6–8

For the béchamel
100 g (3½ oz) salted butter
100 g (3½ oz/scant 1 cup) plain
   (all-purpose) flour
1.2 litres (40½ fl oz/5 cups) whole
   (full fat) milk
20 grinds of freshly ground
   black pepper
⅛ of a nutmeg, grated

For the bolognese
4 tablespoons extra virgin olive oil
6 rashers smoked streaky bacon,
   thinly sliced
2 large onions, peeled and finely
   chopped

2 large carrots, peeled, cut in four
   lengthways and finely chopped
2 hefty celery stalks, cut in four
   lengthways and finely chopped
1 kg (2 lb 4 oz) beef mince
280 g (10 oz) tomato purée (paste)
1 litre (34 fl oz/4 cups) beef stock
1 strip of lemon zest
2 bay leaves
1 good pinch of ground nutmeg

To assemble
Béchamel sauce
10–15 lasagne sheets, depending on the
   size of your dish
150 g (5 oz) Parmesan, coarsely grated

First, make the béchamel. In a heavy bottomed saucepan over a medium–low heat, melt the butter until just frothing. Dust in the flour and whisk to combine, cooking this floury paste out for 4–5 minutes, whisking regularly. Once it starts to smell gently of biscuits and toasty and has darkened in colour, add the milk a little at a time, splash, splash, whisking to a smooth emulsion with each addition. Once about half the milk is in you should have a thick sauce, at this point you can steadily pour in the remaining milk, whisking all the time. Add the pepper and the nutmeg and allow to gently blip away for 3–5 minutes, when a final whisk should reveal a smooth béchamel with the thickness of double (heavy) cream. Remove from the heat and allow to cool.

Next, make the Bolognese. Find a large heavy bottomed pan – a casserole (Dutch oven) would be perfect here. Place the pan over a medium flame and get the olive oil in. Once the oil is hot, add the bacon and move it around with your wooden spoon. Once it's browned a bit, 3–4 minutes, add the onion, carrots and celery. Add a good four finger pinch of salt, give it all a healthy stir and sweat out for 15 minutes, stirring occasionally. Do not skimp on this. That bacon-y residue and the long, slow sweating of your onions etc will give you all the depth of flavour and sweetness this sauce needs.

After 15 minutes, increase the heat and add the mince. Cook until it's mostly brown, around 5–10 minutes. Then add the tomato purée. If your purée was in tins, put some of your beef stock in the empty purée tins and swill it all about – leave no flavour stone unturned.

Add the stock filled tins, the rest of the stock, the lemon peel, the bay leaves and the nutmeg. Bring to the boil and reduce to a slow simmer. Put the lid on and don't touch it much – just checking occasionally that the bottom isn't sticking and lowering the heat if necessary. Cook for 30 minutes, take the lid off, remove the peel and bay and cook at the same gentle pace for at least another 30 minutes. Tend it occasionally and regularly at first to make sure nothing's sticking – you might need to lower the heat a bit. There's never any harm in a cursory stir, a little taste, etc.

While the Bolognese is cooking, blanch the pasta sheets. Bring a pan of salted water to the boil, then lay out a clean tea towel. Drop the pasta sheets them into the pot separately, one by one, and cook in batches of three or four sheets, before fetching them from the water and laying them to dry on the tea towel.

Once you have your blanched pasta sheets, your cooked and cooled béchamel and your bolognese, you are set to build your lasagne.

Preheat the oven to 180°C (350°F/gas 6).

Find a deep large dish (ceramic, enamel, metal is all good, you just want about 5 cm (2 in) of depth and roughly 30 cm x 20 cm (12 in x 8 in) in size). Start by adding a tiny bit of your bolognese to the bottom of the dish and smearing it about, then the first sheets of pasta, then a quarter of your Bolognese, smeared about the place, then quarter of your béchamel smeared about the place, then a layer of pasta. Repeat meat, sauce, pasta for two more layers. Finally, spoon the final quarter of your béchamel over the top of the last layer of pasta, spread it about into a nice layer with the back of your spoon, and cover liberally with the grated parmesan.

Pop the lasagne in the hot oven and cook for 40 minutes until golden brown, bubbly and crispy edged. Leave to sit for 20 minutes to allow the layers to settle and for the molten inside to cool. Cut into generous squares and serve. If picnicking, wrapping the whole thing (or individual portions) in tin foil and tea towels when hot out of the oven will mean you've got a couple of hours to transport it somewhere, and you can still have hot lasagna out and about. And don't forget how good a sliver of this is popped inside a croissant and toasted in a toastie machine or fried in a pan the next day.

HACKS

Six other things that are perfect in a toasted croissant

1 Leftover lasagne or another pasta dish (or any other promising leftovers).

2 Any charcuterie with grated mozzarella.

3 Meat from the Sunday roast, with mustard and leftover gravy.

4 Pastrami, sauerkraut and cheese with French's mustard.

5 Peanut butter with your favourite chocolate bar, all broken up.

6 Biscoff spread with sliced banana and pomegranate molasses.

All left to cool and then taken with you on a day out. If you're tempted to dive straight in, be warned that the contents will be ferociously hot!

Index

ice lollies, Campari, crème de menthe and orange 215
iced tea, perfect 'Arnold Palmer' 42

J

jam: candied marrow and fennel jam 96
  pumpkin and ginger jam 97
Joan Lee's all-day breakfast quiche 25

K

Kewpie mayonnaise: egg salad sandwich 182

L

lager: Michelada 140
lasagne, my mum's 239
leeks: Glamorgan sausages 124
lemon curd: mascarpone, almond butter and lemon curd toasted croissant 241
lemon sorbet: Sgropino Bambino 198
lentils, braised 123
lettuce: the Big Max 226
  seafood cocktail 40
  steak tartare 39
lime juice: Michelada 140
  Running the Gimlet 198

M

macaroons, coconut 63
Malibu: Park Bench Pina Colada 198
marmalade: breakfast martini 110
marrows: candied marrow and fennel jam 96
Marsala: zabaglione with macerated fruit 154
martini, breakfast 110
marzipan: Battenberg cake 64
mascarpone: eight easy-peasy chees(y) cakes 178–9
  mascarpone, almond butter and lemon curd toasted croissant 241
mayonnaise: the Big Max 226
  cocktail sauce 40
  egg salad sandwich 182

schmaltz mayo 83
  six things to mix into 207
meat trifle 209–10
Michelada 140
milkshakes: bourbon 196
  the Wake and Shake 198
mostarda ('mustard fruit') 126
muffins, Ben's infinitely hackable sausage and egg 225
mushrooms: full English breakfast shooter's sandwich 107
  Joan Lee's all-day breakfast quiche 25
my mum's lasagne 239

N

nduja, Taleggio and honey toasted croissant 240
Nick Bramham's amazing ricotta-filled cannoli 66

O

oranges: Campari, crème de menthe and orange ice lollies 215
  fennel salad 168

P

Park Bench Pina Colada 198
pasta: my mum's lasagne 239
  tortellini in brodo 149–51
pastis, perfect 168
pâté, chicken liver 80
  meat trifle 209–10
peppers: gazpacho 137–8
  green chilli – for the perfect hot dog 52
pesce crudo 152
pickles: pickled eggs 26
  pickley fries 194
  six super-lush quick-pickles 223
picnic essentials 29
pineapple juice: Park Bench Pina Colada 198
pork: green chilli – for the perfect hot dog 52
  pork scratchings 184

tortellini in brodo 149–51
potato rolls 54
  green chilli – for the perfect hot dog 52
potatoes: meat trifle 209–10
  pickley fries 194
  potato samosas 181
prosciutto: tortellini in brodo 149–51
prosecco: Sgropino Bambino 198
pumpkin: chicken-stuffed pumpkin 79
  pumpkin and ginger jam 97
punch, Guinness 55

Q
quiche, Joan Lee's all-day breakfast 25

R
ricotta: eight easy-peasy chees(y)
  cakes 178–9
  Nick Bramham's amazing ricotta-filled
    cannoli 66
rum: Guinness punch 55
  Park Bench Pina Colada 198
  the Wake and Shake 198
Running the Gimlet 198

S
salad, fennel 168
salt 29, 165
  salts for boiled eggs 167
samosas, potato 181
sandwiches: egg salad sandwich 182
  full English breakfast shooter's
    sandwich 107
sauces 29
  bechamel sauce 239
  brown sauce, aka picnic gold 28
  cocktail sauce 40
  schmaltz mayo 83
sausages: Ben's infinitely hackable
  sausage and egg muffin 225
  full English breakfast shooter's
    sandwich 107
  Glamorgan sausages 124
  green chilli – for the perfect hot dog 52

Joan Lee's all-day breakfast quiche 25
schmaltz mayo 83
scones, perfect 95
seafood cocktail 40
Sgropino Bambino 198
shooter's sandwich, full English
  breakfast 107
So Nearly Sangria 198
soups: chicken soup 193
  three gazpachos 137–9
Sprite: So Nearly Sangria 198
steak tartare 39
stout: brown sauce, aka picnic gold 28

T
tea, perfect 'Arnold Palmer' iced 42
tomatoes: brown sauce, aka picnic gold 28
  chicken kiev parmo 229
  full English breakfast shooter's
    sandwich 107
  gazpacho 137–8
  Joan Lee's all-day breakfast quiche 25
  meat trifle 209–10
  my mum's lasagne 239
tortellini in brodo 149–51
trifle, meat 209–10

V
vanilla ice cream: bourbon milkshake 196
vodka: Bloody Hell Mary 198
  Sgropino Bambino 198

W
the Wake and Shake 109
wine: meat trifle 209–10
  So Nearly Sangria 198
the world's best hot chocolate 244

Z
zabaglione with macerated fruit 154

About the Authors

Max Halley is a picnicker and sandwich shop owner of some repute, a self-publicist of great repute and Britain's handsomest, buffest press-up champion, by no repute. He occasionally drinks too much and often delivers late, but he loves his mother.

Ben is a devoted eater, cook, and writer, often in that order.

 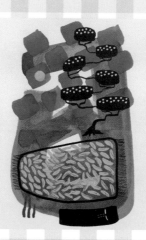 

Disappearing, Why Did Nobody Come to My Banana Picnic and *Sausage Picnic* by Louis Caulfield

Acknowledgements

Ben

To Eve for proving that you can polish a turd.

To Louise, Alex and Sophie, for turning gobbledegook into visual splendor.

To Max for sharing the terrifying inside of your mind with me, and letting me picnic in there with you.

Max

Eve Marleau for putting up with the incessant phone calls and being nothing but wonderful, generous of time and spirit and believing in the thing right from the start.

Laura Willis, Ruth Tewkesbury, Laura Eldridge and all at Hardie Grant for being brilliant, and forgiving!!!

Alexander Breeze, Louise Hagger and Sophie Bronze for the extraordinary photographs, the delicious chocolate brownies and prop based genius.

Evi. O Studio for the gingham bonanza!!!

Araminta Whitley and Marina de Pass for being right there with us on everything.

Mama, Dada and Lydia for being a group of absolute LEGENDS and keeping the emotional wolf from the door.

Himesh Patel, Louis Caulfield, Mark Sadler and Reuben Dangoor for generous, and excellent contributions.

Neil Gill and Jamie Green for encouragement right from the start.

The Newbolt Family (and Hannah), for help, encouragement, wine, Scrabble Club and a place to rest my head.

Holly Chaves, Joe Hall and Milly Mouse.

James Pamphlion, Dre 'The Dog' Stylianou, Tom 'The Enforcer' Mcsweeney, William Matthews, Isaac Lee-Kronick and Joe Beeching for everything and being total, utter LEGENDS!!!

Johnny The Window-Cleaner for the years of love, diligent window cleaning, and entertaining phoning of extremely suspicious people on the Sandwich Shop landline and my mobile phone.

Dani Reid & Joe Mackertich because I spelt your names wrong last time and you're total ballers!!!

Chris Hassell, for all the plans, unending support and serious lunches.

Falco and Ray for the Pipes and The Sparks.

Coralie Sleap, for being a joy.

Kat and Merry, Elsie, Arthur and George for being a family away from family and a home away from home.

Simon Rimmer, Tim Lovejoy, Charlie Critchfield, Alice Riley and Paddy Ruddy (and all at Sunday Brunch!!!!!) for the bants, the LOLS and CHANGING THE GAME!

Owen, Hanna and Matilda for the sausages and everything.

Claudia and Eloise for being wonderful breaks in the rain.

Rosie Hobbs for sorting me out with the flat and welcoming me to the neighbourhood.

Ethan Davids for the lager tops, chewing the fat and becoming friends.

Gavin Singleton for the amazing website and years of help.

Fay Maschler and Itamar Srulovich – Ocelots FOREVER.

Francesca Pearce for her extraordinary work on The Sandwich Book.

Nick Trower from the estimable Biercraft and all the years of help.

Ben Benton for love, support, utter-brilliance and getting stuff done like no one else.

Everyone who has ever been to the Sandwich Shop, watched me being silly on the internet, TV or wherever, bought a Sandwich Book or been any support in any way!! THANK YOU FOR EVERYTHING!

XXXXXXxxxxxxxxxxxxxxxxxx

Published in 2021 by Hardie Grant Books,
an imprint of Hardie Grant Publishing

Hardie Grant Books (London)
5th & 6th Floors
52–54 Southwark Street
London SE1 1UN

Hardie Grant Books (Melbourne)
Building 1, 658 Church Street
Richmond, Victoria 3121

hardiegrantbooks.com

British Library Cataloguing-in-Publication Data.
A catalogue record for this book is available from the British Library.

Max's Picnic Book by Max Halley and Ben Benton
ISBN: 978-1-78488-421-5

10 9 8 7 6 5 4 3 2 1

Publisher: Kajal Mistry
Commissioning Editor: Eve Marleau
Design: Evi-O.Studio | Evi O. & Nicole Ho
Photographer: Louise Hagger
Food Stylists: Max Halley and Ben Benton
Prop Stylist: Alexander Breeze
Copy-editor: Alison Cowan
Proofreader: Tara O'Sullivan
Indexer: Vanessa Bird
Production Controller: Nikolaus Ginelli

Colour reproduction by p2d
Printed and bound in China by Leo Paper Products Ltd.